The most difficult subjects can be explained to the most slow-witted man if he has not formed any idea of them already;

But the simplest thing cannot be made clear to the most intelligent man if he is firmly persuaded that he knows already, without a shadow of doubt.

Leo Tolstoy (1897)

Dedicated to:

My wife, Carolyn,

Our sons, Doug and Rich,

Their wives, Joyce and Erika,

Our grandchildren,

Tyler, Callie, Brett, Chase

Justin, Brennan and Connor

And to all of the generations they represent.

Equity Press

Copyright © 2010 by Richard C. Huseman

Library of Congress Cataloging-in-Publication Data

Relational Intelligence® is the registered trademark of PRISM, Inc., a Richard C. Huseman company

Photos courtesy of Shutterstock.com

Cover design by Aaron Holck at Emagination Unlimited, Inc.
www.emaginationunlimited.com

Huseman, Richard C.
Man-made global warming hoax: how a lack of relational intelligence® has allowed fraudulent science & our government to cost American taxpayers billions of dollars already… and possibly trillions more.

Richard C. Huseman, Ph.D.
p.   cm.

ISBN: 978-0-9841525-2-0
1. Global Warming   2. Cap and Trade   3. Relational Intelligence®
4. Human Thought   5. Human Perception   6. Ethanol   7. Science
8. Tax spending

PRINTED IN THE UNITED STATES OF AMERICA

ACKNOWLEDGEMENTS

Any book project is always the effort of several people. This book is no exception. First, I wish to give credit where credit is due. The original inspiration for this book came from listening to Rush Limbaugh's radio show. Many years ago, Rush was among the first, perhaps **THE** first, to question man-made global warming. His statements put me on a path of intense study to research and inform myself about the subject, decide to write this book. On numerous occasions, Rush referred to man-made global warming as a hoax. When I checked the dictionary for the definition of hoax, I found the following:

HOAX /HOŪKS/

1. *something intended to deceive or defraud (i.e., The Piltdown man was a scientific hoax.)*
2. *to deceive by a hoax; hoodwink.*
3. *something that has been established or accepted by fraudulent means.*

So, as usual, Rush had nailed it by using the term "hoax" in reference to man-made global warming and I had a title for my book. So, thank you Rush.

I wish to thank my colleague, Dr. Martin Stickley. Not only is Martin a good friend but also a fellow believer in the hoax that is man-made global warming. Martin was kind enough to share with me his materials on alternative views about global warming, which he presented to the U.S. Chamber of Commerce in Washington, D.C. in early 2009. Martin has also been kind enough to read piece-meal sections of the book from time to time during its development, and he gave me helpful feedback and suggestions about the material we presented. I am deeply grateful for Martin's input and support.

Both in my academic and corporate life, I have had the opportunity to author several books, including this one. While I might be responsible for the content and message of these books, for the last several years, I have relied on someone else to actually get the ideas down on paper. This person not only formats the books and creates most of their graphics, she has also drafted portions of this manuscript and made many suggestions about how to make the content readable and engaging. Thank you, Zulema Seguel.

Another great help for this book has been my research assistant, Cyndi Beltran. Her assistance in pulling together the background research for this book, and her attention to detail with the documentation and sourcing of all the materials, has been invaluable.

No book can go to print without having a careful eye check that all the "t's" are crossed and all the "i's" are dotted; not to mention the correct use of punctuation and grammar. For her exceptionally detailed proofing efforts, I wish to thank, Kerry Novick.

Last, but certainly not least, I wish to thank my wife, Carolyn. Over the years, she has seen me through many book projects – 15 in all. She is the one who keeps these projects moving forward. From gentle hints of "How's it going?" to sometimes more forceful pushes of "Let's get this thing done," her encouragement and support always keeps me moving forward. Thanks, Han.

CONTENTS

part three | THE CONSEQUENCES OF THE MAN-MADE GLOBAL WARMING HOAX 91

FOREWORD

Al Gore and many others (at one earlier point, 84% of the population) believe that man-made global warming is one of, if not THE MOST SIGNIFICANT ISSUE THE WORLD FACES. The purpose of this book is to put man-made global warming in proper perspective. The ability to put ideas and concepts into proper perspective is one of the most powerful abilities mankind possesses. However, that ability is frequently in short supply, especially when it comes to man-made global warming.

As the author, I need to clarify that I am not a climatologist or a scientist from any related field of science. I am not an economist, nor am I a politician. I am a concerned citizen; one that in his over 40 years in academe and corporate America, has had many opportunities to try and discern truth from fiction on a myriad of issues. From my days as a debate coach at the University of Georgia, to the executive offices and boardrooms of some of the world's largest corporations, I have learned the danger of seeing only one side of an issue. As difficult as it sometimes is, there is great value in questioning not only how others come to their conclusions, but how we come to our own.

In my roles as a debate coach, professor and executive coach, I REALIZE A LARGE PART OF WHAT I DO IS HELP PEOPLE THINK BETTER. You can throw data and information at people all day long, but unless you encourage them to THINK about what you are telling them, you are just wasting your time. How do you get people to think better? You present information in novel and interesting ways, allowing them to see things from a different perspective. You ask them questions to inspire them to look at why and how they believe what they believe. Most importantly, you give people an opportunity to embrace new information and make it their "own" so that they enhance their own Relational Intelligence® about an issue or idea.

That is the real purpose behind this book. Man-made global warming is the issue I've chosen to feature because of its critical economic and social impact on our country and our world, but I could have written a similar book on any number of topics from welfare to health care. Why? Because it is the same lack of RELATIONAL INTELLIGENCE® on the part of the government and most of the public (see chapter two) that allows these issues to be misunderstood by so many.

But, for this book, it is the man-made global warming hoax that is the focus, and it is my intention to help people wake up to the realities of how much bad information is being disseminated about this issue. I want them to think differently about what they are being told about this issue. The science shared in this book is summarized from the work of many well-respected scientists. The data has come from the most reliable sources I have been able to find. The perspective is mine, and it is a perspective that I believe the issue of man-made global warming desperately needs.

THE POWER OF PERSPECTIVE

In their book, **Super Freakonomics**, Steven Levitt and Stephen Dubner tell a story that provides a compelling parallel to our current situation regarding man-man global warming, which we have paraphrased below:

> When the world was lurching into the modern era, it grew more populous, and in a hurry. Most of this expansion took place in urban centers like London, Paris, New York and Chicago. In the United States alone, cities grew by 30 million residents during the nineteenth century, with a half of that gain in just the final 20 years.
>
> But as this swarm of humanity moved itself, and its goods, from place to place, a problem emerged. The main mode of transportation produced a slew of unintended consequences, including gridlock, high insurance costs, and far too many traffic fatalities. Crops that would have landed on a family's dinner table were sometimes converted into fuel, driving up food prices and causing shortages. Then there were the air pollutants and toxic emissions, endangering the environment as well as individuals' health.
>
> We are talking about the automobile – right?
>
> Not so fast. We are talking about the HORSE.
>
> The horse, a versatile and powerful helpmate since the days of antiquity, was put to work in many ways as modern cities expanded: pulling streetcars and private coaches, hauling construction materials, unloading freight from ships and trains, even powering the machines that churned out furniture, rope, beer and clothing. When a fire broke out, a team of horses charged through the streets with a

pumping truck. At the turn of the twentieth century, some 200,000 horses lived and worked in New York Citt; one horse for every 17 people.

But oh, the unintended consequences!

Horse-drawn wagons clogged the streets, and when a horse broke down, it was often put to death on the spot. This caused further delays. Many stable owners held life-insurance policies that, to guard against fraud, stipulated the animal be euthanized by a third party. This meant waiting for the police and/or a veterinarian to arrive. Even death didn't end the gridlock. "Dead horses were extremely unwieldy," writes the transportation scholar Eric Morris. "As a result, street cleaners often waited for the corpses to putrefy so they could more easily be sawed into pieces and carted off."

The noise from iron wagon wheels and horseshoes was so disturbing – it purportedly caused widespread nervous disorders – some cities banned horse traffic on the streets around hospitals and other sensitive areas.

*And it was frighteningly easy to be struck down by a horse or wagon, neither of which is as easy to control as they appear in the movies, especially on slick, crowded city streets. **In 1900, horse accidents claimed the lives of 200 New Yorkers, or one in every 17,000 residents. In 2007, meanwhile, 274 New Yorkers died in auto accidents, or one of every 30,000 residents.** This means that a New Yorker was nearly twice as likely to die from a horse accident in 1900 than from a car accident today.*

*Worst of all was the **dung**. The average horse produced **about 24 pounds of manure a day. With 200,000 horses, that's nearly 5 million pounds of horse manure. A day.** Where did it go?*

*Decades earlier, when horses were less plentiful in cities, there was a smooth-functioning market for manure, with farmers buying it to truck off (via horse, of course) to their fields. But as the urban equine population exploded, there was a massive glut. In **vacant lots, horse manure was piled as high as sixty feet.** It lined city streets like banks of snow. In the summertime, it stank to the heavens; when the rains came, a soupy stream of horse manure flooded the crosswalks and seeped into people's basements. Today, when you admire old New York* *brownstones and their elegant stoops, rising from street level to the second-story parlor, keep in mind that this was a design necessity, allowing a homeowner to rise above the sea of horse manure.*

*All of this dung was terrifically unhealthy. It was a breeding ground for billions of flies that spread a host of deadly diseases. Rats and other vermin swarmed the mountains of manure to pick out undigested oats and other horse feed – crops that were becoming more costly for human consumption thanks to higher horse demand. **No one at the time was worried about global warming, but if they had been, the horse would have been Public Enemy No. 1, for its manure emits methane, a powerful greenhouse gas.***

In 1898, New York hosted the first international urban planning conference. The agenda was dominated by sessions on horse manure, because cities around the world were experiencing the same crisis. But no solution could be found. "Stumped by the crisis," writes Eric Morris, "The urban planning conference declared its work fruitless and broke up after three days instead of the scheduled ten."

The world had seemingly reached the point where it's largest cities could not survive without the horse, but couldn't survive with it, either.

***And then, the problem vanished.** It was neither government action nor divine intervention that did the trick. City dwellers did not rise up in some mass movement of altruism or self-restraint, surrendering all the benefits of horse power. The problem was solved by **private enterprise**. No, not the invention of the dung-less animal. The horse was kicked to the curb by the electric streetcar and the automobile, both of which were much, much cleaner and far more efficient. **The automobile, cheaper to own and operate than a horse-drawn vehicle, was proclaimed "an environmental savior."** Cities around the world were able to take a deep breath – without holding their noses at last – and resume their march of progress.*

The story, unfortunately, does not end there. The solutions that saved the twentieth century seem to have imperiled the twenty-first, because the automobile and electric streetcar carried their own unintended consequences. The carbon emissions spat out over the past century are claimed by climate cultists to have warmed the Earth's atmosphere. Just as equine activity once threatened to stomp out civilization, there is now a fear the human activity will do the same. MARTIN WEITZMAN, an environmentalist at Harvard, argues that there is roughly a 5 percent chance that global temperatures will rise enough to "effectively DESTROY planet Earth as we know it."

This is perhaps not very surprising. When the solution to a given problem doesn't lay right before our eyes, it is easy to assume that no solution exists. But history has shown again and again that such assumptions are wrong. Mankind has a great capacity for finding technological solutions to seemingly intractable problems, and this will likely be the case for global warming.

OH, BY THE WAY, THE VALUE OF HORSE MANURE, INCIDENTALLY, HAS REBOUNDED, so much so that the owners of one Massachusetts farm recently called the police to stop a neighbor from hauling horse manure away. The neighbor claimed there was a misunderstanding, that he'd been given permission by the farm's previous owner. But the current owner wouldn't back down, demanding 600 dollars for the manure.

WHO WAS THIS MANURE-LOVING NEIGHBOR? NONE OTHER THAN MARTIN WEITZMAN, THE ENVIRONMENTALIST AT HARVARD WITH THE GRAVE GLOBAL WARMING PREDICTION CITED ABOVE.

One colleague wrote to Weitzman when the story hit the papers. "MOST ENVIRONMENTALISTS I KNOW ARE NET EXPORTERS OF HORSESHIT. YOU ARE, IT SEEMS, A NET IMPORTER. CONGRATULATIONS!"

Looking back, it is easy to smile while reading this story. But, at one time, horse shit was a problem that nearly paralyzed urban America. In a few years, it is this author's hope that people will read the stories about man-made global warming and the massive initiatives that were launched by the government in its name, and find the tale just as laughable. But, given the high-cost consequences that will be the result of man-made global warming initiatives, the end of the story may not be anywhere near as funny.

This book was written to be as readable and readily accessible as possible. While this book is rooted in sound science and fact (as the end notes at the end of the book will show), it is also meant to be entertaining and certainly, thought-provoking.

IF YOU ARE IN AGREEMENT THAT MAN-MADE GLOBAL WARMING IS A HOAX, then this book will provide you with evidence you can use to help lead others to the truth, as well. **IN FACT, WE HAVE PROVIDED A SUMMARY OF THE MAJOR ARGUMENTS OF THIS BOOK IN A QUESTION AND ANSWER FORMAT IN APPENDIX A OF THIS BOOK.** This has been done in order to help those who want to get and spread the truth about the man-made global warming hoax in a succinct and persuasive way.

IF YOU ARE A MAN-MADE GLOBAL WARMING BELIEVER, this book will provide an eye-opening look as to the **REAL** truth behind how little man can and does affect global temperatures. More importantly, this book will hopefully awaken your Relational Intelligence® about the issue of man-made global warming, and how it is being used as pretext for a government takeover of the energy industry.

Richard C. Huseman, Ph.D.

MAN-MADE GLOBAL WARMING

HOAX

part one | THE PROBLEM AT HAND

The first part of this book is dedicated to giving a brief overview of the issue of MAN-MADE GLOBAL WARMING and how it has been perpetuated through a lack of Relational Intelligence® on the part of scientists, the government and the American public.

RELATIONAL INTELLIGENCE® is the key to really understanding the facts about man-made global warming. Throughout this book, we will attempt to increase your RQ regarding man-made global warming by providing what we call "RQ INSIGHTS." RQ Insights are about looking at data and information in new ways... perhaps in ways unlike how you have viewed them in the past. As a result, you may choose to come to different conclusions... sometimes dramatically different conclusions about global warming and the significance of the role man plays in affecting global temperatures.

CHAPTER ONE |
THE MAN-MADE GLOBAL WARMING ISSUE

At the core of the issue set forth by "man-made global warming" enthusiasts is the assertion that there is AN UNNATURAL INCREASE IN GLOBAL TEMPERATURES. This increase, according to the warming advocates, is caused NOT BY NATURAL — BUT UNNATURAL INCREASES IN CARBON DIOXIDE (CO_2), AND THAT THESE INCREASES ARE PRODUCED BY MAN.

The issue of man-made global warming is an unequaled example of the manipulation and, in some cases, outright falsification of information. In addition, given the tremendous amount of information provided by reputable scientists that global warming is NOT ACTUALLY CAUSED BY MAN, it is quite remarkable that the notion of man-made global warming has persisted for decades.

This book will show without a shadow of a doubt that the miniscule amount of carbon dioxide emitted by man into the atmosphere DOES NOT contribute in any significant way to global warming. Yes, there have been periods of warming and cooling of Earth's temperatures throughout history, but these warming and cooling periods are NOT CAUSED BY MAN.

However, beyond the argument of the accuracy of the science of man-made global warming, there is a much more urgent issue. As a country, the United States has already spent billions of dollars on research projects and advertising campaigns to support the idea of MAN-MADE global warming. Indeed, there are some "scientists" who have built their entire careers securing "research" grants from the federal government to prove the concept of man-made global warming, and predict the dire consequences of its effects.

However, far more sinister and far more costly, is our government's plan to institute a policy of "CARBON DIOXIDE EMISSION CAP & TRADE" that will cost trillions of dollars more as we continue the pointless battle against MAN-MADE global warming. Not only will we be turning over significant control of the energy industry to the government, but, the financial consequences of global warming will be staggering to every individual on this planet.

WARMING NOT POLLUTION

To be clear, this book argues against the concept of man-made global warming – not all environmental causes as a whole. Primarily due to the media and a lack of understanding on the part of the general public, "global warming" has become an all encompassing term. For instance, in the eyes of many, smog is a man-made global warming issue. THIS IS NOT TRUE! Smog in many of our larger cities, as well as hazardous chemicals being dumped in our rivers and streams, oil spills, etc. are all dangerous forms of SURFACE POLLUTION. THERE IS NO EVIDENCE THAT SURFACE POLLUTION HAS ANY INFLUENCE ON CLIMATE AND THESE ISSUES ARE NOT RELATED TO MAN-MADE GLOBAL WARMING.

Man DOES produce surface pollution, and over the years we have made good progress in dealing with it. With some exceptions, most of our streams and rivers are cleaner than they once were. But more can and needs to be done. SURFACE POLLUTION IS WHERE WE NEED TO FOCUS OUR CONCERN FOR THE ENVIRONMENT.

Do not be misled. All of the money and effort related to combating man-made global warming, such as the reduction of carbon dioxide emissions, DOES NOT address issues of surface pollution. CARBON DIOXIDE (CO_2) IS NOT SMOG. CO_2 is odorless, tasteless, invisible, and as we will show later in this book, has very little influence over our climate. In fact, RATHER THAN A FORM OF POLLUTION, CO_2 IS VITAL FOR FOOD PRODUCTION AND LIFE ITSELF!

Before we move on to more details about the man-made global warming hoax, let's briefly look at how the man-made global warming cause came into being.

A BRIEF HISTORY OF MAN-MADE GLOBAL WARMING

Ian Plimer in his book, **Heaven and Earth**, notes that global warming got its start as early as 1827 when a man named Josephe Fourier suggested that the atmosphere traps heat radiated by the sun. Later in 1860, John Tyndall identified a group of gases called "greenhouse gases" (primarily water vapor but also carbon dioxide, methane and other miscellaneous gases) as responsible for trapping the heat of the sun's rays. Then a little later, near the turn of the century, a chemist by the name of Svante Arrhenius boldly stated that if the concentrations of only one "greenhouse gas" – carbon dioxide – were to double, GLOBAL TEMPERATURES WOULD RISE 5 DEGREES CENTIGRADE! Arrhenius' "forecast" was completely wrong but it was too late. The CO_2 train had pulled out of the station!

Then, Guy Challender in 1938 stated that warming, which was occurring in the 1930's, could be caused by the release of CO_2 in the atmosphere FROM HUMAN ACTIVITY! Challender and others were the ones who first made the case for MAN-MADE global warming. The outbreak of World War II, of course, led to major increases in industrial production. This industrialization and its continuation after the war produced increases in CO_2 emissions. BUT DESPITE CHALLENDER'S PREDICTIONS, global temperatures DID NOT RISE. Instead temperatures DECLINED. We had a cooling period that lasted approximately 35 years between 1940 and 1975.

THE SEVENTIES ICE AGE

By the mid-seventies, after experiencing a much colder winter in the United States, tides had turned to such a degree that rather than worrying about global warming, many media outlets warned of a coming "ICE AGE." For example, on June 24, 1974, *Time* magazine ran a feature article on the coming ice age. The excerpt from the *Time* article that follows, has a familiar theme, as do many articles appearing today. ONLY 35 YEARS AGO, WE WERE BEING TOLD THAT WE WOULD FREEZE TO DEATH, not die from overheating.

> However widely the weather varies from place to place and time to time, when meteorologists take an average of temperatures around the globe they find that the atmosphere has been growing gradually COOLER for the past three decades. The trend shows no indication of reversing. Climatological Cassandras are becoming increasingly apprehensive, for the weather aberrations they are studying may be the harbinger of another ice age.
>
> Telltale signs are everywhere... MAN, TOO, MAY BE SOMEWHAT RESPONSIBLE FOR THE COOLING TREND. The University of Wisconsin's Reid A. Bryson and other climatologists suggest that dust and other particles released into the atmosphere as a result of farming and fuel burning may be blocking more and more sunlight from reaching and heating the surface of the earth.

Newsweek printed a similar article on April 28, 1975. **National Geographic** followed suit shortly thereafter. About that time, much of the mainstream media hyped the ideas as set forth by Lowell Ponte in his 1975 book, **The Cooling: Has the Next Ice Age Already Begun?** Ponte stated in his book:

"This cooling has already killed hundreds of thousands of people. If it continues and no strong action is taken, it will cause world famine, world chaos and world war, and this could all come about by the year 2000."

Ponte's book was endorsed by a climatologist named STEPHEN SCHNEIDER who said:

"This well written book [The Cooling] points out in clear language that the climatic threat could be as awesome as any we might face, and that massive worldwide actions to hedge against that threat deserve immediate attention."

In a bizarre twist, only one decade later toward the end of the 1980's, the same STEPHEN SCHNEIDER who endorsed Ponte's book on global cooling, wrote his own book. This book, printed in 1989, was titled, **Global Warming**. Wow! TALK ABOUT A REVERSAL. Schneider did a major 180° as did many others. In a span of only a few years, "science" was able to swing their predictions from one extreme (A COMING ICE AGE) to the other (A THREAT OF GLOBAL WARMING).

The incredible part of this pendulous change in belief was that, in the mid 1970's, large numbers of scientists came out with absolute conviction that the "Ice Age" data was valid and that the consequences to our planet would be dire. Many "Ice Age" supporters stuck to their guns long after contrary data became prevalent. The same can be said about man-made global warming enthusiasts today. There is an ever-growing mountain of scientific data proving that MAN-MADE global warming is a fallacy, yet support for the cause continues. How is this possible? How is the man-made global warming hoax being perpetuated?

A HOAX IN PERPETUITY?

There are four major reasons why the man-made global warming hoax is continuing to be perpetuated. Three of these reasons are as follows:

- ⊙ Political advantage
- ⊙ Protection of scientific credibility through scientific tribalism
- ⊙ Media manipulation

RQ Insight

At the peak of the consensus,
84 PERCENT of Americans believed
global warming was a threat.

The only thing they agreed on more
was the existence of God.

1. Political Advantage

Man-made global warming provides a tremendous political rallying cry. Our national and economic security is more and more intricately intertwined within a global community. As a result, finding an enemy across the shore that can galvanize Americans to a cause is more and more difficult. However, a climatic problem which threatens everyone, no matter their ideological or political beliefs, provides a far stronger unifying force. UNDER THE BANNER OF MAN-MADE GLOBAL WARMING, OUR GOVERNMENT AND ITS LEADERS HAVE BEEN ABLE TO PUSH OUT POLICIES WITH OVERWHELMING PUBLIC SUPPORT, EVEN IF THOSE POLICIES HAVE SIGNIFICANT NEGATIVE CONSEQUENCES.

These days, any piece of legislation, both in the U.S. and abroad, that in any way addresses the "threat" of man-made global warming, has an almost free ride to pass. Because of the issue's overwhelming public support, elected officials who dare to oppose man-made global warming legislation face censure from their constituents. Being dubbed "environment haters" (or deniers), legislators who hold strong against ill-advised, costly and futile policies can even find their incumbency endangered for going up against the massive man-made global warming force.

Meanwhile, other policy-makers continue to foster and leverage man-made global warming for their own purposes. Consider both the Kyoto Accord and more recently, the Copenhagen Climate Conference. If the policies either from Kyoto or Copenhagen were actually implemented, they would greatly weaken the economy in the United States and other developed countries. Third world countries would be deprived of using coal, a relatively cheap source of energy, and thus unable to build the industries that would allow them to escape their third world status. ONLY POLICY MAKERS THEMSELVES WOULD PROFIT FROM THEIR OWN GLOBAL WARMING LEGISLATION EITHER THROUGH GAINING MORE CONTROL OVER THE ENERGY INDUSTRY, THROUGH THEIR CORPORATE LIAISONS, OR THROUGH THEIR PERSONAL INVESTMENT IN GLOBAL WARMING TECHNOLOGIES.

Man-Made Global Warming Goes Global

In 1988, always looking for causes to support its existence, THE UNITED NATIONS ESTABLISHED THE INTERGOVERNMENTAL PANEL ON CLIMATE CHANGE (IPCC). The establishment of the IPCC played a major role in creating a worldwide focus on man-made global warming. In 1989, the United States Senate opened hearings on man-made global warming, chaired by then-senator Al Gore. GORE, first with his book, **Earth in the Balance**, then later his movie, **An Inconvenient Truth**, and culminating with his Nobel Peace Prize for saving mother earth, BECAME THE KEY INDIVIDUAL IN GALVANIZING SUPPORT FOR THE MAN-MADE GLOBAL WARMING

CRUSADE. As we will show later, Al Gore stands to make massive financial gains from the man-made global warming legislation he proposes. He and many other political leaders have a vested financial interest in keeping the man-made global warming hoax alive and valid in the minds of the American public. The political and financial advantage to be gained from perpetuating the global warming hoax is behind much of the continued campaigning being done as part of the cause.

2. PROTECTION OF SCIENTIFIC CREDIBILITY THROUGH SCIENTIFIC TRIBALISM

Over the past several years, scientists from every country and a variety of disciplines have thrown their weight behind the man-made global warming cause. They have put their credibility on the line in order to find back up data that shows that man's use of hydrocarbon fuels has increased carbon dioxide emissions to the point that the Earth is heating up unnaturally. These scientists, often recipients of hefty grants from our universities and government, went out in search of more and more data proving their man-made global warming hypotheses correct. The problem is many times the data wouldn't cooperate. More and more often, these scientists discovered that their findings ran contrary to man-made global warming rhetoric. But, at this point, many were individually and collectively so committed to the man-made global warming cause, that they couldn't afford to back away. Their research monies and continued credibility hinged upon finding the "right" data.

Remember the scientist who initially endorsed the global cooling book and then ten years later wrote his own book about global warming: STEPHEN SCHNEIDER? In his book, he wrote about what he calls his "ALARMIST STRATEGY." He stated that scientists need to be "aggressive" to gain support for man-made global warming. Schneider's own words are quite revealing.

> "On the one hand as scientists, we are ethically bound to the scientific method... we need to get some broad-based support to capture the public imagination... to get loads of media coverage... we have to offer some very scary scenarios... [and] make little mention of any doubts we might have... EACH OF US HAS TO DECIDE WHAT THE RIGHT BALANCE IS BETWEEN BEING EFFECTIVE AND BEING HONEST." [emphasis added]

Schneider's incredible statement highlights the ethical issue currently alive in the man-made global warming debate. As an ever increasing amount of data comes out proving man-made global warming a hoax, scientists must choose between being discredited for their earlier statements in support of the cause, or forced to continue defending a dying crusade. Those who continue to defend man-made global wagons are circling the wagons and pointing their media-loaded guns outward in an attempt to discredit contrary data and the scientists who stand behind it. This scientific tribalism forces a continued debate on an issue that should have long since been put to rest. The man-made global warming hoax has been revealed, but its legacy lives on thanks to those pseudoscientists who refuse to give up the pointless fight.

NEWS FLASH…NOT ALL SCIENTISTS SUPPORT MAN-MADE GLOBAL WARMING

Not all scientists have signed on to the man-made global warming band wagon. Actually, there are thousands of scientists who do not support MAN-MADE global warming. So, how is it that only now we are beginning to hear their opposition? There are at least two reasons:

1. Reputable scientists are GOOD AT THEIR CRAFT AND GOOD AT COMMUNICATING WITH EACH OTHER. What they are not so good at is COMMUNICATING WITH THE PUBLIC, ESPECIALLY THE MASS MEDIA.

2. On the other hand, SOME NOT SO REPUTABLE "SCIENTISTS" and their academic institutions have honed their communication skills with the public, and have teamed up with spokesmen like AL GORE. They have greater access to the mass media and work diligently to silence any opposing opinions.

One of the leaders in the fight against man-made global warming is DR. ARTHUR ROBINSON, a research professor of chemistry and co-founder of the Oregon Institute of Science and Medicine. Dr. Robinson, in a February 2010 article in the **Whistleblower**, succinctly explains the situation.

> Is the custom and culture within the American academic institutions in which [American scientists] work conducive to the free flow of information between our best scientists and public? **NO. THESE INSTITUTIONS HAVE BEEN CO-OPTED BY THEIR DEPENDENCE ON GOVERNMENT TAX FUNDS.**
>
> Can we rely upon news reports that tell us the newly reported finding of American scientists? **NO! A VERY LARGE GROUP OF PSEUDOSCIENTISTS IS NOW PRESENT AMONG OUR SCIENTISTS, AND IT IS THOSE WHO SEEK AND RECEIVE MOST OF THE PUBLICITY BROUGHT TO US BY OUR PRINT AND TELEVISION MEDIA.**
>
> Are our best scientists blameless in this? **AGAIN, NO. THEY HAVE WATCHED PASSIVELY AS THEIR PROFESSION, WHICH DEPENDS UPON ABSOLUTE HONESTY, IS REPRESENTED BY DISHONEST PEOPLE IN PUBLIC FORUMS — AND MANY HAVE NOT**

SPOKEN IN OPPOSITION TO THESE MISREPRESENTATIONS. If they permit this to continue, the inevitable backlash will eventually come. When that happens, the true scientists will suffer right along with the pseudoscientists – a reward they will both richly deserve. (emphasis added)

3. THE MEDIA PLAYS TO OUR "CATASTROPHIC MINDSET"

The human brain developed during a time when staying alive was the first priority for our earliest ancestors. Back in the Pleistocene Era, hominid brains were on constant alert to ensure survival: securing food and water, finding protection from the elements, and more importantly, staying alert for predators and other dangers. Hominid brains were programmed to seek out POTENTIAL CATASTROPHE at every moment and around every corner.

You might pity our hominid ancestors and their "CATASTROPHIC BRAIN," but their programming was the key to our successful existence and continuation as a species. But, despite the millions of years that have passed between their existence and our own, our brains still carry much of the same catastrophic wiring. WE HAVE A BUILT IN TENDENCY TO FEAR THE WORST SCENARIO WILL HAPPEN.

Excellent evidence of this catastrophic wiring is how the media attracts our attention today. Disaster, death, threats to safety and security, all trigger our catastrophic brains to pay attention, and we become riveted to what the media presents as the latest potential dangers to our continued existence. THE FACT THAT MANY OF US FEAR WE ARE CAUSING OUR OWN DEMISE THROUGH MAN-MADE GLOBAL WARMING IS A PERFECT EXAMPLE OF HOW THE MEDIA CAN MANIPULATE US INTO KEEPING THEIR SUBSCRIPTION, WEB HITS, AND VIEWERSHIP RATES UP. Every article or broadcast about how man-made global warming threatens our survival will receive guaranteed attention because of our "catastrophic brain."

THE FINAL REASON

In addition to the political advantage, scientific tribalism and the media hype sustaining the man-made global warming campaign, there is one final reason that the man-made global warming hoax has persisted for decades in spite of scientific evidence to the contrary. In this author's opinion, it is the most important and the most troubling reason that many falsehoods continue to flourish with the general public's and our government's support. It is people's LACK OF RELATIONAL INTELLIGENCE® about man-made global warming (and other issues) that has allowed the hoax to persist as long as it has. In the next chapter, we will set forth the concept of RELATIONAL INTELLIGENCE®. We will illustrate how low levels of

RELATIONAL INTELLIGENCE® enable many people to cling to the idea that man-made global warming exists and is a major threat to mankind.

CHAPTER TWO |

THE LACK OF RELATIONAL INTELLIGENCE® REGARDING MAN-MADE GLOBAL WARMING

You know about IQ (how smart you are). You may have heard of EQ (your emotional intelligence). **HAVE YOU HEARD OF RQ (YOUR RELATIONAL INTELLIGENCE®)?**

THE FOUNDATION OF RELATIONAL INTELLIGENCE®

In the 1960's, a group of psychologists began looking at how the brain perceived and evaluated risks. Their discoveries led to the emergence of a new body of science focusing on the psychology of judgment and decision-making, behavior economics and hedonic psychology. Chief among those breaking ground in this new psychological territory was Daniel Kahneman, a professor of psychology at Princeton University. Kahneman and his colleague, Amos Tversky, developed a realistic model for predicting how people make choices in situations where they have to decide between alternatives involving risk, such as financial decisions. Kahnemnan's **PROSPECT THEORY**, despite the fact that he purportedly never took an economics course in his life, won him the 2002 Nobel Memorial Prize in Economics "for having integrated insights from psychological research into economics, science, especially concerning human judgment and decision-making under uncertainty."

The work of Kahneman and other psychologists focus on the idea that the human brain had not one but two systems of thinking, a belief similarly held by ancient Greek philosophers who assigned the two types of thought to two gods – Dionysius and Apollo. In modern times, Kahneman simply refers to the two systems of thinking as System One and System Two.

SYSTEM ONE IS INTUITION. It is fast, automatic, parallel, effortless, associative, slow-learning and emotional. People find it difficult to explain decisions based on intuition and, sometimes, don't even realize that they actually made a decision. Their choice is so instinctive that, to them, there is no choice at all.

SYSTEM TWO IS REASON. Reason is deliberate, controlled, effortful, rule-governed, flexible and emotionally neutral. Most importantly, **ONCE A DECISION BASED ON REASON IS REACHED, IT CAN BE PUT INTO WORDS, EXPLAINED AND LATER MODIFIED IF NEW EVIDENCE IS PRESENTED.**

A CLOSER LOOK AT INTUITION

For our purposes, it is System One (intuitive thinking) that holds particular interest. Unlike reason, intuition operates WITHOUT our conscious awareness. It is not reflective, but incredibly fast. According to Kahneman, intuition is responsible for both marvels and illusions. The good thing about intuition, while it takes a long time to form, is that it is often quite accurate. The bad thing about intuition is that it can not only be erroneous, but also "the errors are very difficult to correct."

Consider for a moment anyone who has worked a particular job for a long period of time. Over the years, these individuals develop a sort of mastery of being able to not only predict potential problems arising from their work, but also able to make quick decisions about how to either prevent or resolve issues. Experienced firefighters, for example, learn over time how to size up the risk of a particular fire, and decide almost instantly how to respond to a blaze. It is almost as if they "know" how a fire will think and act. Psychologists call this "recognition-primed decision making" or more simply, their past experience has allowed them to form a strong intuitive ability for how to react to a similar, current situation. If asked, these firefighters would find it difficult to explain exactly how and why they make the decisions they make. They simply recognized what needs to be done and do it with little "thought" involved.

Let's take a more personal look at intuitive thinking. Imagine you are staying at a large hotel in a major city. You ask the concierge to recommend a restaurant for dinner. You then walk the five blocks to the restaurant. It is early in the evening and the streets are bustling with people. You arrive at the restaurant, have a glass of wine, and eat dinner. After dinner, as you leave the restaurant, the maitre d' asks if you would like a cab. You politely decline and say you would prefer to walk. Once outside you quickly notice that the streets are now empty of other pedestrians, and are poorly lit. Halfway down the first block, you see a homeless man asleep in a doorway. Then, in the distance, you see three dangerous looking figures come toward you on the sidewalk. Suddenly, you turn around and quickly head back to the restaurant and tell the maitre d' you would like to take him up on his offer to call you a cab. He smiles, and fifteen minutes later you are in the cab heading back to your hotel.

What just happened? Did you just become aware of the latest robbery and murder statistics for this particular city? No. Something in your gut told you this was not the safest place for an after dinner walk – IT WAS AN AUTOMATIC RESPONSE. WHEN SYSTEM ONE IS IN PLAY, YOU ARRIVE AT A JUDGMENT LIGHTNING FAST, AND AT USUALLY A SUBCONSCIOUS LEVEL, AND FREQUENTLY ARE UNABLE TO EXPLAIN OR PUT INTO WORDS WHY YOU MAKE THE DECISIONS YOU DO.

INTUITION IS A TWO-EDGED SWORD

Intuitive thinking, while allowing you to make a judgment in a split second, is also flawed because it can lead you to IRRATIONAL CONCLUSIONS. Intuition comes from the most ancient part of our brain, the part that protected us from getting eaten by wild animals who thought we might make a good lunch. While human experience has taken some of what was inherited and greatly added to it, much of the ancient brain remains today. But, unlike our ancestors, modern man does not spend much time hunting mammoths and escaping from carnivorous beasts – situations that required "reaction" not "reflection." So, today while there are still occasions where intuitive thinking serves us well and protects us from danger, there are many cases where our intuition can get us into trouble, especially when we make decisions without giving them much thought.

For example, consider the problem below:

> A bat and ball cost 11.00 dollars. The bat costs ten dollars more than the ball. How much does the ball cost?

If you are like 50 percent of the Princeton undergraduates Kahneman has tested (and a slightly lower percentage of MIT students), your reflexive answer would be, "one dollar." You might want to recheck your "reasoning." One dollar might be the intuitive answer, but if you gave the problem a bit more thought, you would realize the correct answer – fifty cents.[1] The error, Kahneman argues is due "LIGHT MONITORING" of the mind.

Interestingly, the people who answer one dollar often argue against the correct answer. They become so tied to their original intuitive response, that they don't allow themselves to take the time to reason out the truth of the answer. HUBRIS, IT TURNS OUT, IS INTUITION'S

---

[1] THE SECRET TO THE CORRECT ANSWER IS TO PAY ATTENTION TO THE WORDING. IF "THE BAT COSTS TEN DOLLARS MORE THAN THE BALL," THE COST OF THE BAT ALONE IS TEN DOLLARS MORE THAN FIFTY CENTS (THE BALL). THUS THE BAT WOULD COST TEN DOLLARS AND FIFTY CENTS WHICH, ADDING THE COST OF THE BALL (FIFTY CENTS), WOULD EQUAL ELEVEN DOLLARS.

GREATEST SIN. Intuitive thinking has a tendency to have us pair very poor accuracy with blazing confidence. "People are poor at assigning weight to evidence," Kahneman observed in his studies of political and economic forecasting. Intuition is resistant to education and, as Kahneman argues, those in intuition's thrall, "HAVE LITTLE ABILITY TO LEARN FROM THEIR MISTAKES."

It is this resistance to new information and reeducation that allows man-made global warming to continue to hold sway in the minds of many people. Over and over again, people have been told that it is man's actions that are causing global temperatures to rise "unnaturally" to the extent that it has now become part of their intuitive programming. Most people do not make the effort to consciously access their SYSTEM TWO/REASON side of their decision-making process on this issue. WHEN IT COMES TO MAN-MADE GLOBAL WARMING, THE DECISION HAS ALREADY BEEN MADE. MAN IS DESTROYING THE EARTH AND WE MUST DO EVERYTHING WE CAN TO STOP THIS FROM HAPPENING… REGARDLESS THAT MORE AND MORE EVIDENCE THAT IS REVEALED TO THE CONTRARY.

The solution is to bring more awareness to how our mental and emotional processes impact how we relate to things around us – individual people, groups, and concepts/ideas like man-made global warming. Taking with us the understanding of how our two systems of thought – intuition and reason – impact our decision-making processes, it is now time to take a serious look at how we can become smarter about our relationships on multiple levels. It is time to assess our own RELATIONAL INTELLIGENCE®.

RELATIONAL INTELLIGENCE® DEFINED
The essence of Relational Intelligence® is captured in the following definition:

> **RELATIONAL INTELLIGENCE®** IS THE ABILITY TO PERCEIVE AND MENTALLY PROCESS DATA, INFORMATION, ASSESS RISK AND PERCEIVE CAUSE AND EFFECT IN WAYS THAT ENABLE YOU TO LEARN, GAIN INSIGHT AND CAPITALIZE ON THE DYNAMICS OF RELATIONSHIPS AT BOTH **MICRO** AND **MACRO** LEVELS.

Before addressing how poor RELATIONAL INTELLIGENCE® has led to the perpetuation of man-made global warming, first let us take a closer look at the concept of Relational Intelligence® itself.

Relational Intelligence®
The Current Interaction

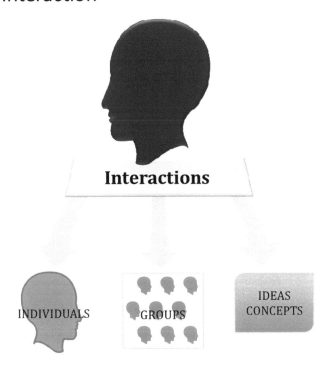

Interactions

INDIVIDUALS   GROUPS   IDEAS CONCEPTS

RELATIONAL INTERACTION PROFILES

There are three broad categories of relationships in which our interactions impact almost every aspect of our lives: one-on-one individual relationships, group relationships and relationships with ideas/concepts. Of the three categories, one operates at the micro level, and two and three function at the macro level. The level of intelligence we exhibit in all of these varied relationships is the measure of how successful we are in our lives.

ONE-ON-ONE INDIVIDUAL RELATIONSHIPS (MICRO LEVEL)

These are the multiple relationships we have with other individuals like our spouse, family members, friends, co-workers, neighbors, etc. These relationships can be intimate or peripheral to our lives (the relationship with your spouse as opposed to your auto mechanic). They can be short-term or long-term (your first grade teacher versus your brother or sister). They can encompass either frequent or infrequent interactions (your co-workers versus your dental hygienist). In each case, your behavior and actions within these relationships have a direct impact on the other individual and the relationship as a whole.

GROUP RELATIONSHIPS (MACRO LEVEL)

These are the relationships we have with the various groups in our lives: our work organization, our church, a favorite sports team, our political party, our neighborhood, our community, etc. Groups also include broader associations like race, gender, age or nationality.

Our group relationships operate on two levels: both our individual relationship with the group, and our relationship to the outside world as a member of the group. For instance, if you are a police officer who volunteers your time to talk to school children about the dangers of drugs, your interactions with the school, the children, their parents and the community will reflect positively on the relationship with the "police" group as a whole. Similarly, if one of your fellow officers is accused of wrong-doing of any kind, it reflects poorly on the group as a whole, including yourself.

RELATIONSHIPS WITH IDEAS/CONCEPTS (MACRO LEVEL)

These are relationships we have with our own view of the world around us. Our views on morality, justice and liberty are all examples of relationships we have with concepts. Our positions on issues like gun control, immigration, education or man-made global warming are all examples of our relationships with ideas. Our relational "interactions" with concepts and ideas are not always as direct as our interactions with individuals or groups. Interaction in this sense refers to how we process new information about something we already have a formed opinion about, how we articulate our position on an issue, or how we reflect on our position during a dilemma or crisis.

RELATIONSHIPS OVER TIME

The core of RELATIONAL INTELLIGENCE® is understanding that all of the relationships you are involved in – be they with individuals, groups or ideas/concepts – evolve over time. Every relational interaction we have is actually three-in-one.

1. **The Relational Prologue:** the history of all past interactions that have occurred in a relationship.
2. **The Current Relational Interaction:** the issues and dynamics at play within the context of the interaction at hand. The key to Relational Intelligence® is understanding all of the elements impacting a current interaction and making conscious decisions of how you want to move forward.

Relational Intelligence® (RQ)

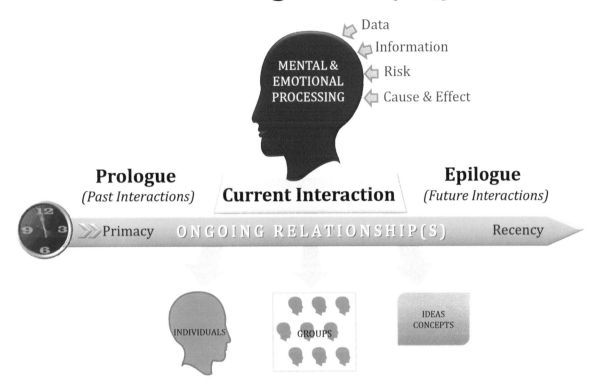

3. **The Relational Epilogue:** the impact that the current interaction, as well as all past interactions, will have on future interactions in the ongoing relationship.

Have you ever been in a situation where an individual's reaction to something you said or did was far more volatile than the situation would justify? THESE EXCESSIVE REACTIONS ARE USUALLY NOT AN ACCURATE REFLECTION OF THE SITUATION AT HAND, but rather a result of accumulated past interactions you have had with that individual or group (the Relational Prologue for that relationship).

Similarly, how you behave in a current interaction will either positively or negatively affect the future of that relationship (the Relational Epilogue). If you are argumentative with a co-worker or supervisor, it will have serious repercussions on the future of your relationship with that individual at work.

THE PROBLEMATIC PROLOGUE

IT'S OUR PROLOGUE THAT OFTEN GETS US INTO TROUBLE. For example, imagine you have a friend and your prologue of interactions with that friend has been very positive. Then suddenly, your friend begins to engage in negative or even harmful behavior. It might take you longer to see the behavior for what it really is. Since you have had only positive interactions with your friend in the past, you are more likely to view your friend's current negative behavior as aberrant.

In group relationships, an example would be if your prologue of interactions with physicians has been positive, you might be more willing to give a current physician the benefit of the doubt during a negative interaction. On the flip side, if you have had a series of negative encounters with attorneys, it may be difficult for you to realize that the lawyer you are meeting with at the moment is very competent and honest.

WHEN IT COMES TO IDEAS/CONCEPTS, take the example of man-made global warming. If your RELATIONAL PROLOGUE was watching Al Gore's *An Inconvenient Truth* movie and all of the weather related disasters, hurricanes, tornados, icebergs breaking apart, drowning polar bears, etc., it will impact how you view information about similar environmental and weather events in the future. For some, the prologue of man-made global warming is so strong that they CAN EVEN VIEW MAJOR BLIZZARDS AS "EVIDENCE" OF WARMING. The media coverage of man-made global warming has created such strong relational prologues that some people can dismiss the fact that since 1998 WE HAVE ACTUALLY BEEN IN A SLIGHT COOLING PERIOD.

THE END OF AN EPILOGUE

There does come a point in some relationships when the only epilogue for the relationship is how it will end. Be it an individual relationship with a friend you have simply lost touch with over time, or a decision to quit a sports team or take another job with a new company, or releasing an old idea or concept you once held dearly (like a belief in Santa Claus)... some relationships need to end. Eventually, enough negative interactions are included in a relational prologue that we realize that we need to fundamentally reevaluate and end a relationship. Unfortunately, in some cases, we wait far too long to see that a relationship is no longer good for us.

RELATIONAL INTELLIGENCE®: ADMIRAL KIMMEL'S STORY

In 1941, Admiral Kimmel, commander in chief of the Pacific fleet, was repeatedly warned about the possibility of war with Japan. On November 24, he was informed that a surprise attack could occur in any direction. However, Kimmel didn't think the United States was in any great danger, and since Hawaii was not specifically mentioned in the report, he took no precautions to protect Pearl Harbor. On December 3, he was told that American cryptographers decoded a Japanese message ordering their embassies around the world to destroy "MOST OF THEIR SECRET CODES." Kimmel focused on the word "MOST" and thought that if Japan was going to war with the United States, they would have

ordered "ALL" their codes destroyed. One hour before the attack on Pearl Harbor, a Japanese sub was sunk near the entry to the harbor. Instead of taking immediate action, Kimmel waited for confirmation that it was, in fact, a Japanese sub. As a result, sixty warships were anchored in the harbor, and planes were lined up wing-to-wing, when the attack came. The Pacific fleet was destroyed and Kimmel was court-martialed. Our desire to cling to an existing belief in the face of contradictory evidence can have disastrous effects. Kimmel's story dramatically illustrates the disastrous results of a lack of RELATIONAL INTELLIGENCE® (i.e., an inability to connect the dots about how his relational prologue was preventing him from seeing the truth about information currently at hand).

It is our contention that one of the major reasons man-made global warming persists is a low level of Relational Intelligence® on the part of the American public, as well as most of our elected officials, including President Obama. Now, don't get me wrong, there are plenty of smart people out there (i.e., people with high IQs). BUT, A NUMBER OF STUDIES HAVE PROVEN THAT IQ ACCOUNTS FOR ONLY 4 TO 10 PERCENT OF CAREER SUCCESS. IQ is not nearly as important as we used to think. When it comes to man-made global warming, RQ is what is all important in understanding the relationships between all the different data points. RQ IS VERY IMPORTANT IN ENABLING A PERSON TO ACCURATELY PERCEIVE CAUSE AND EFFECT IN THE MAN-MADE GLOBAL WARMING ARENA.

RELATIONAL INTELLIGENCE® AND HOW YOUR BRAIN ACTUALLY FUNCTIONS

Earlier we defined RELATIONAL INTELLIGENCE® as the ability to perceive and mentally process data and information in ways that enable us to learn, understand, and leverage the dynamics of relationships at both micro and macro levels. Focus on the first part of the definition; "THE ABILITY TO PERCEIVE AND MENTALLY PROCESS DATA AND INFORMATION." Seems easy, doesn't it? But, what appears to be a straight forward process is actually quite complicated. Remember the work done by Daniel Kahneman about the two systems of thought: feeling and reason? In order to gain some insight and understanding regarding RELATIONAL

INTELLIGENCE®, we need to explore how our brains apply these two systems of thought within relationships.

Our brains are extremely complex and powerful. Our brain, however, cannot process all the information that continually bombards it. So, in order to cope, our brains develop the ability to:

- ○ Add in information
- ○ Edit out information
- ○ Rearrange information to fit our existing mindsets

These three abilities allow our brains to quickly filter huge amounts of information in a way that we can efficiently process it. Without them, we could easily find ourselves completely overwhelmed by the world around us. However, while these abilities are major assets to us, they can also have their drawbacks. We will look at each in turn to see how some of our greatest mental strengths can sometimes limit our ability to perceive things accurately.

THE BRAIN ADDS-IN INFORMATION

Sometimes, our brain causes us to add-in information that, in actuality, isn't there. For example, what do you see below?

Most people would respond something like "a pie with a slice taken out of it" or perhaps "a Pacman." Now, consider the next image. What do you see now?

Do you see three "Pacmen?" So far, so good. Now it gets a little more complicated when you turn the page.

Let's try one more. What do you see below?

Do you see five Pacmen... or do you see a five-pointed star? You really shouldn't see a star because, in actuality, there is no star. There is just empty space between five colored shapes. Your brain "added-in" a star because it recognized a pattern that it already had wired into it from past experience.   In fact, the ability for the brain to add-in information is so strong that the "star" actually appears whiter and brighter than the white paper outside the "star." What you see above is actually just five Pacmen arranged in a circle. When it comes to man-made global warming, the same can be said. As we will prove in later chapters, the data that suggests that man is responsible for global warming is just like the star... NOTHING BUT EMPTY SPACE.

THE BRAIN EDITS-OUT INFORMATION

Sometimes, the brain edits out new information because it doesn't fit into an existing pattern. By way of an example, read the words below out loud. Ready? Go.

When you
wish upon a
a star

What did you say? Was it "When you wish upon a star" If you think so, check again. Keep checking until your brain "sees" what it most likely previously omitted. HAVE YOU FOUND THE SECOND "A"? Most of us are wired so that we don't see the second "a" in the image. We edit it out as if it weren't there. And, we do this all the time with information coming into our brains without ever realizing it.

THE BRAIN CAN REARRANGE INFORMATION TO MEET EXPECTATIONS

Sometimes, the brain takes new information and shuffles it around to fit into a pattern we are familiar with. For example, can you make out the sentence below?

> *We mkae sesne of waht we "pierceve" oistude of orusevlses in lgrae prat baesd on the pearttns of wniirg we hvae inidse our midns.*[2]

This interesting phenomenon was reportedly first discovered in a study at Cambridge University and has become known as TYPOGLYCEMIA.   According to the study, people can read perfectly any text as long as the FIRST and the LAST letters maintain their respectful positions. It doesn't matter if all the other letters in the word are mixed up, as long as the first and last letters are in the right place, PATTERN RECOGNITION IN THE BRAIN ALLOWS US TO "READ" THE WORD CORRECTLY.

You see, the brain has been programmed to recognize most of the words we read without actually needing to process every letter. It recognizes the pattern of words by their "frame" of the first and last letter, and by the basic length of the word. The middle letters, whatever their order, aren't as important to our recognition ability as the first and last letters. The first and last letters tell us what we should expect to see... the brain REARRANGES the rest according to existing patterns. Now, if the brain can do this within the relatively simple process of reading, **thnik** about how your brain might be rearranging other new and far more important information to meet its pre-programmed expectations (say in regard to man-made global warming). The brains ability to add in information, edit out information, and rearrange information, results in what is called COGNITIVE CONSISTENCY SYNDROME.

---

[2] HERE IS THE UNSCRAMBLED VERSION OF THE SENTENCE ABOVE. "WE MAKE SENSE OF WHAT WE "PERCEIVE" OUTSIDE OF OURSELVES IN LARGE PART BASED ON THE PATTERNS OF WIRING WE HAVE INSIDE OUR MINDS."

RQ Insight

The bad news is that after your teenage years, your IQ remains relatively **UNCHANGED** throughout your life.

RQ (Relational Intelligence®), on the other hand, **CAN BE GREATLY IMPROVED VIA SELF-AWARENESS THROUGHOUT YOUR ENTIRE LIFE.**

Cognitive Consistency Syndrome

All of us selectively process information by READILY ACCEPTING WHAT CONFIRMS/CONFORMS TO OUR CURRENT BELIEFS AND SYSTEMATICALLY IGNORE OR DISTORT INFORMATION THAT IS CONTRARY TO OUR BELIEFS. COGNITIVE CONSISTENCY SYNDROME (CCS) is a tendency for people to seek out and/or interpret information that confirms their preconceptions (prologue) or beliefs, independently of whether the information is true. People reinforce their existing attitudes by selectively collecting new evidence, by interpreting evidence in a biased way, or by ignoring the information altogether. All of us tend to test our beliefs in a one-sided way, focusing on one possibility and frequently failing to examine alternatives.

COGNITIVE CONSISTENCY SYNDROME can lead to disastrous decision-making, especially in organizational, military and political contexts. COGNITIVE CONSISTENCY SYNDROME contributes to overconfidence in existing personal beliefs and an unwillingness or, at times, an inability to view information with any kind of real objectivity. IT IS A MAJOR REASON PEOPLE BELIEVE AND CONTINUE TO BELIEVE IN MAN-MADE GLOBAL WARMING.

Once you have developed a bit of a mindset (perhaps after you watched Al Gore's movie) regarding man-made global warming, you are very likely to systematically seek out information to support your view (mindset) and screen out other information that does not support your view.

Emotions & their impact on how the brain processes information

In the examples you just read, you may have discovered how the brain can misinterpret and distort even relatively simple information because of how your brain is wired. But these distortions tend to become greatly amplified when you add EMOTIONS to the mix.

Consider the following four questions:

Question 1: How many people in the United States die each year of skin cancer? Approximately 9,600 – yet many of us continue to sunbathe.

Question 2: How many people in the United States die each year in auto accidents? Approximately 40,000 (with 3,189,000 people injured) – yet 86 percent of the population that is 15 years and older has driver's licenses.

Question 3: How many people in the United States die each year of diseases related to smoking? More than 430,000 – yet approximately 46.2 million Americans continue to smoke (with 3,000 young people becoming new smokers every day).

Question 4:   How many swimmers die each year from shark attacks WORLDWIDE?   The average for the new millennium is three deaths per year worldwide!

Armed with these statistics, the next time you are near the ocean, walk down to the beach and gingerly step over all the people lying there soaking up the sun's rays and scorching their skin. Wade into the surf until it gets about knee-high. THEN, AT THE TOP OF YOUR LUNGS, YELL TWO WORDS… "SHARK! SHARK!" Then stand back and watch all of the people…

- ○ Scramble out of the water
- ○ Stumble over the sunbathers
- ○ Jump into their cars
- ○ Light up a cigarette
- ○ And, drive to "SAFETY"

OK, you know you won't actually try this little experiment, but you get the point. People are susceptible to what we call "Shark Syndrome Perception." Despite having a finely tuned capacity for understanding the world around them, people often perceive only what they want to about their surroundings, no matter what the facts are, and despite the efforts of reasonable people to convince them otherwise. Why? Sharks are scary creatures. They seem much more foreboding than cigarettes or cars. Even though the risk in reality is very small (three deaths per year worldwide), our EMOTIONAL reaction galvanizes our perception of sharks. We have a much stronger "emotional reaction" to sharks… even though cars and cigarettes pose a far greater risk to us.

Let's look at this in another way. Which animal potentially frightens you more: a GREAT WHITE SHARK or an ELEPHANT? Again, despite our earlier clarification about shark deaths, most people would pick the great white. Why? Because in our childhood, many of us saw movies or read books about loveable elephants like Dumbo and Barbar. Either that, or we watched in awe as elephants lumbered about doing tricks in circus rings. We weren't taught to be afraid of elephants. Yet, ELEPHANTS KILL AT LEAST 200 PEOPLE EACH YEAR! In this case, our positive emotions outweigh the reality of the situation. Because most of elephant related deaths are in remote areas and receive little to no media coverage, we remain blissfully ignorant of the danger. Elephants are powerful and sometimes volatile creatures, and yet the great white shark is far more feared. If sharks had any legal representation at all, they should have sued the makers of the movie, *Jaws*.

A BIT LATER IN THIS BOOK, YOU WILL SEE HOW AL GORE AND THE MAN-MADE GLOBAL WARMING ALARMISTS HAVE SKILLFULLY ENGAGED OUR EMOTIONS WHEN IT COMES TO POLAR BEARS, PENGUINS, RISING OCEANS, HURRICANES, FAMINES, ETC. IN THEIR ATTEMPT TO CONVINCE THE PUBLIC OF THE "DANGERS" OF MAN-MADE GLOBAL WARMING. But, first, let's look at one more emotional element that can have a major impact on our ability to reason effectively.

THE BLAME GAME

ANYTIME WE FEEL DISCOMFORT IN ANY FORM, IT IS INSTINCTIVE FOR US TO DO EVERYTHING IN OUR POWER TO IMMEDIATELY IDENTIFY THE CAUSE SO THAT WE CAN ALLEVIATE THE DISCOMFORT. If we feel an uncomfortably cold draft, we immediately seek out the source. If someone bumps into us, we quickly turn to see who it is. This elemental instinct to identify the cause of discomfort is the foundation for the psychology of blame. Blaming is nearly universally observed in children and is an essential part of human development. As humans, we are extremely sensitive to circumstances that are either potentially or in actuality harmful to us. Similarly, we are sensitive to instances where our own actions potentially or actually cause harm to others. This is the flip side of blame; guilt. BLAME AND GUILT ARE EXTREMELY POWERFUL EMOTIONS THAT HAVE A DECIDED IMPACT ON OUR RELATIONAL INTELLIGENCE®.

For example, imagine that there is a gas that kills 20,000 people a year in the European Union and another 21,000 people a year in the United States. This imaginary gas is a by-product of industrial processes, and scientists can precisely identify which industries, even which factories, are emitting the gas. Finally, imagine that all of these facts are widely known but no one – not the media, not environmental groups, not the public – is all that concerned.

Sound like an absurd scenario? Well, it is not. It is not an imaginary gas but a very real one; one that really is the second leading cause of lung cancer in the United States after smoking, and the leading cause of lung cancer in non-smokers. Do you know what it is? It is RADON.

Radon is a radioactive gas that can cause lung cancer if it pools indoors at high concentrations, which it does in regions that scientists can identify with a fair degree of precision. RADON KILLS AN ESTIMATED 41,000 PEOPLE A YEAR IN THE UNITED STATES AND THE EUROPEAN UNION. Public health agencies routinely run awareness campaigns about the danger, but journalists and environmentalists have seldom shown much interest and the public, it's fair to say, has only a vague notion of what this stuff is.

So, why are people so indifferent to a gas that is far more dangerous to their health than man-made global warming could ever be? The reason is that there is NO ONE TO BLAME. RADON IS PRODUCED NATURALLY in some rocks and soils. THE DEATHS IT INFLICTS ARE SOLITARY AND QUIET AND NO ONE APPEARS TO BE PERSONALLY RESPONSIBLE. The same people who shake at the knees at the idea of radiation from sources like nuclear waste dumps or the "dangers" associated with man-made global warming consider radon – which is an incontrovertible killer – a very low risk. Nature kills, but nature is hard to BLAME. We can shake our fists at volcanoes all day long, but it won't make any difference. The absence of outrage is the reason that natural risks are far more accepted than man-made dangers.

THE ISSUE OF MAN-MADE GLOBAL WARMING IS A PERFECT EMOTIONAL ONE-TWO-PUNCH. First, you get hit from the right because you can blame oil companies, irresponsible factory owners, the people who drive alone in the carpool-only lanes, etc. Then, you get jabbed from the left because you can also feel guilty about how you contribute to man-made global warming whenever you get into your non-hybrid SUV, or forget to turn off the lights in your house when you go out.

When it comes to man-made global warming, the way our brain EDITS IN information, EDITS OUT information, and REARRANGES information, together with the use of a wide VARIETY OF EMOTIONAL APPEALS INCLUDING BLAME AND GUILT, it becomes very difficult to discern the truth from the fiction about whether man actually has any impact on global temperatures.

WHEN THE RELATIONALLY INTELLIGENT TRY AND TALK TO THE MASSES

Without a high degree of Relational Intelligence®, we fail to make intelligent decisions about new information we receive. LIKE A FRIEND WE HAVE KNOWN FOR MANY YEARS, WE GIVE MAN-MADE GLOBAL WARMING THE BENEFIT OF THE DOUBT AND DON'T SEE IT FOR WHAT IT REALLY IS… A LIE PERPETUATED BY FRAUDULENT SCIENTISTS, OUR GOVERNMENT, THE MEDIA, AND OURSELVES. This low Relational Intelligence® results in continued belief and support for the man-made global warming cause, a cause whose fight will continue to have devastating results on our economy and on our lives.

Aided by scientists and the media, our government has created an economic, political, social and cultural tsunami that makes it very difficult for anyone to even attempt to view contrary opinions on man-made global warming. If you even try to question the accepted truth of man-made global warming, you are quickly labeled as selfish, arrogant and/or uncaring about the future of our planet and the human race. Global warming has become like politics and religion, an issue best left out of polite conversation unless everyone in the room shares similar viewpoints (as you can imagine, this author has caused some uncomfortable moments when out to dinner with friends, in some cases, now former friends).

The danger with the current blind commitment to man-made global warming policies is that many people are no longer willing to consider the mountain of data that argues to the contrary. They can't see that the government could be spending the billions it intends to invest into this issue in other, far more beneficial ways. Voters laud their political officials for putting their names to any type of bill with the term "man-made global warming" in it, regardless of what is actually in the bill. Thus, with their cause justified and supported by the majority of American people, the government has free rein to push their agenda further, once again without recognizing the potential harmful consequences their policies will have. THE GOVERNMENT'S LACK OF RELATIONAL INTELLIGENCE® WHEN IT COMES TO GLOBAL WARMING IS NOT ONLY STUNNING, BUT DANGEROUS AND RIDICULOUSLY EXPENSIVE. IT IS ONLY SURPASSED BY THE PUBLIC'S UNWILLINGNESS TO LOOK AT THEIR OWN RELATIONAL INTELLIGENCE WHEN IT COMES TO MAN-MADE GLOBAL WARMING.

Author's Note

PLEASE UNDERSTAND THAT IT IS **NOT** THIS AUTHOR'S POSITION THAT WE SIMPLY IGNORE THE ENVIRONMENT IN OUR RUSH TO CREATE A BETTER LIFE FOR OURSELVES. IT IS OUR RESPONSIBILITY AS STEWARDS OF THE EARTH TO UTILIZE RESOURCES WISELY, DO WHAT WE CAN TO PROTECT OTHER SPECIES AND LEAVE AS LITTLE OF AN ENVIRONMENTAL FOOTPRINT BEHIND AS POSSIBLE. WE CAN AND SHOULD TAKE STRIDES TO CONTINUE TO REDUCE SURFACE POLLUTION. HOWEVER, MAN IS NEITHER RESPONSIBLE FOR NOR ABLE TO AFFECT GLOBAL WARMING. THE ISSUE RELEVANT TO THIS BOOK IS THAT OUR GOVERNMENT HAS BASICALLY **INVENTED A CAUSE TO JUSTIFY THE POLICIES THEY WANT TO PUT INTO ACTION, TO COLLECT TRILLIONS IN ADDITIONAL TAXES AND TAKE CONTROL OF THE ENERGY INDUSTRY.**

CHAPTER THREE |

AL GORE – THE CLIMATE GOD?

MAN-MADE GLOBAL WARMING IS A HOAX!

That is correct! **MAN-MADE GLOBAL WARMING IS A HOAX! IT IS AN IDEOLOGICAL AGENDA MASQUERADING AS SCIENTIFIC THEORY.** Let me explain. Al Gore and other man-made global warming enthusiasts would have you believe that human-kind's current use of fossil fuels is responsible for such a drastic increase in greenhouse gases that it is causing the temperature of the Earth to rise to dangerous levels, threatening the oceans, weather patterns, animal species and our own existence. **FOR HIS EFFORTS, AL RECEIVED THE 2007 NOBEL PEACE PRIZE "FOR MAKING PEACE WITH MOTHER EARTH."** Note that Al Gore did not receive a Nobel Prize for Science! But, Hollywood did reward Gore's slideshow, *An Inconvenient Truth*, with two Academy Awards. As we will show shortly, Al knows very little about science, especially the "science of man-made global warming."

There is absolutely no real data to substantiate Al's position. The data that has been presented to the public has been skewed, often deliberately, to reinforce the government's propaganda message about the issue. In some cases, contrary data has actually been omitted. Let's look at several key elements of the "man-made" global arguments and see how the real scientific evidence dramatically proves the contrary.

OH, BY THE WAY, AL GORE DID NOT INVENT THE INTERNET BUT...

Nobel Peace Prize Laureates Al Gore (left) and R. K. Pachauri, Chairman of the Intergovernmental Panel on Climate Change (IPCC) with their Nobel Peace Prize Medals and Diplomas at the Award Ceremony in Oslo, Norway, 10 December 2007. Photo: Ken Opprann

Al Gore

Did Invent

"MAN-MADE"
Global Warming

Al Gore is the biggest reason global warming has become the colossal issue it is today. At first, he blatantly leveraged his political office to push the government's global warming agenda into people's homes, both locally and internationally. In his movie, *An Inconvenient Truth*, data was manipulated with one intent: to frighten people to fall in line with the government's global warming agenda. When the movie came out, education leaders insisted that it be played in classrooms. Frightened children went home to their parents and threw fits if their parents didn't recycle more, buy more expensive "green" household products, trade-in their gas-guzzlers for more fuel efficient cars, and do anything else they could to save the cute little polar bear cubs and their mommies. Many schools also strongly suggested parents come to school and watch the movie with their children.

Not taking drastic action to correct global warming will be catastrophic. We'll be eight degrees hotter in ten years and basically none of the crops will grow. Most of the people will have died and the rest of us will be CANNIBALS.

Ted Turner,
April 2, 2008

It wasn't just schools. The media and big name celebrities quickly started rallying around the man-made global warming cause. Consider the statement made by Ted Turner above. Really! It is hard to believe an educated individual could make such an ill-conceived statement as, "Global warming will turn us into CANNIBALS." Yet many other celebrities have made unfounded, sometimes silly statements, as well.

AL GORE'S MASSIVE CARBON "FOOTPRINT"

In his movie, *An Inconvenient Truth*, Al Gore offers several suggestions for how people can help the global warming cause. They should start within their own home by purchasing energy-efficient lighting, appliances, and get an energy audit to make sure their homes are being cooled and heated efficiently. IF ONLY AL WOULD TAKE HIS OWN ADVICE. The Tennessee Center for Policy Research actually performed an energy audit on the former vice president's home and reported the following results on Al's energy efficiency.

The average household in America consumes 10,656 kilowatt-hours (kWh) per year, according to the

Department of Energy. *IN 2006, GORE DEVOURED NEARLY 221,000 KWH – MORE THAN 20 TIMES THE NATIONAL AVERAGE!*

In August alone, Gore burned through 22,619 kWh – *GUZZLING MORE THAN TWICE THE ELECTRICITY IN ONE MONTH THAN AN AVERAGE AMERICAN FAMILY USES IN AN ENTIRE YEAR!*

Since the release of *An Inconvenient Truth*, Gore's energy consumption has increased from an average of 16,200 kWh per month in 2005 to 18,400 kWh per month in 2006.

Gore's extravagant energy use does not stop at his electric bill. Natural gas bills for Gore's mansion and guest house averaged 1,080 dollars per month last year.

When confronted with this data, Gore's office made the following official incredible comment:

> The bottom line is that every family has a different carbon footprint. And what Vice President Gore has asked is for families to calculate that footprint and take steps to reduce and offset it."

As for why their boss doesn't practice what he preaches was never answered. It was, however, pointed out that the former vice president does "offset" his greenhouse emissions. An offset is when you pay a firm to somehow neutralize your emissions (by planting trees or paying other developing countries not to emit so much CO_2). Sounds good but, of course, this means that there has to be a twist. HIS OFFSETS COME FROM GENERATION INVESTMENT MANAGEMENT (GIM), THE COMPANY HE HIMSELF FOUNDED! DOES HE PAY FOR THESE OFFSETS? OF COURSE NOT! THEY ARE SIMPLY PART OF AL'S BENEFITS PACKAGE!

Gore's Tennessee mansion is only one of many properties he owns. He has a house in Northern Virginia and a condo in San Francisco – on the waterfront (I guess Al isn't really all that worried about rising sea levels resulting from man-made global warming). The latest addition to his real estate holdings is an ocean-view villa on 1.5 acres in Montecito, California that Al bought in April 2010. This nearly nine million dollar Italian style house has a swimming pool, spa, fountains, SIX FIREPLACES (for those cold California winters), five bedrooms and NINE BATHROOMS. One can only guess at how big Al's carbon footprint really is but it seems it is getting larger and larger.

PRACTICE WHAT YOU PREACH

"This issue of global warming is going to impact every single person. It's not a political issue, it's a moral issue. Global warming is happening right now, and... we are causing it. We are impacting the climate. Humans have become a force of nature themselves, and the impacts are going to be horrific if we don't do something about it."
— Laurie David

Laurie David flew on a private jet to Texas A&M campus to give a speech about the importance of changing **INDIVIDUAL BEHAVIOR TO FIGHT GLOBAL WARMING**. By the way, she also flies privately between her home in Los Angeles and her 25,000 square foot home in Martha's Vineyard, a home in which she was issued a "notice of apparent violations" for building a 26-foot-long barbecue station, a stone and concrete bonfire pit, and an outdoor theater on an environmentally sensitive patch of property... without the proper permits! When confronted about her hypocrisy, Ms. David responded:

"I feel horribly guilty about it. I probably shouldn't do it. But the truth is, I'm not perfect... I don't expect anybody else to be perfect either. That just pushes people away."

OH, BY THE WAY, LAURIE DAVID IS A GLOBAL WARMING ACTIVIST AND THE PRODUCER OF AL GORE'S MOVIE, *An Inconvenient Truth*.

AN END TO MARITAL BLISS MEANS MORE CARBON EMISSIONS

If divorce wasn't difficult enough for couples, there is now an added element of concern. Never mind breaking up a family and permanently damaging all parties involved (especially children), research now shows that DIVORCE CAUSES GLOBAL WARMING! According to a recent study from Michigan State University (MSU), divorced families have significantly larger carbon footprints than non-divorced families. Distinguished Professor and Chair of Ecological Sustainability at MSU's Center for Systems Integration and Sustainability, Jianguo Liu, discovered the "inconvenient truth" while surveying domestic situations across the United States and 11 additional countries including Brazil, Ecuador, Kenya, Mexico and Spain. Liu and his team of researchers found that family splits consistently lead to hefty surges in transportation, construction and consumption.

It makes perfect sense. Divorce most often ends in dual residences. And we all know that housing sprawl is not good for the environment. (According to calculations by Architecture 2030, a nonprofit organization supported by the American Institute of Architects and the U.S. Green Building Council, the residential building sector is responsible for 21 percent of all greenhouse gas emissions).

With so many families moving from one residence to two, it's no wonder the environmental impact is intense. According to the U.S. Census, the year 2000 saw the addition of six million "extra" households from divorce. Now, let's do the math . . . double the resources to build the house, twice the fuel to heat, cool and run the house, and twice the provisions (cars, can openers, Fido and Spot, the pet dog and cat).

To pour some salt in the wound, split households have fewer people in them, yet they use close to the same amount of energy as a full house. For example, a refrigerator uses roughly the same amount of energy whether it runs for a family of four or for a single dad eating microwaveable TV dinners. On a per-capita basis, divorced residents consume more goods, use more electricity and water, and thus contribute to the emission of more greenhouse gases than those families who live in a single dwelling. It all harks back to the simple principles of resource allocation and efficiency. Two houses, a rented apartment across town, weekdays with mom, weekends with dad, and every third Monday dinner at your maternal grandmother's. Divorce isn't easy for anyone... especially the environment.

Finally, let's not forget all the environmental damage of celebrity splits. Though a miniscule portion of the population, celebrity divorcees wreak eco-havoc. First, there are those carbon emissions: jetting off to the Dominican Republic for a quickie annulment takes fuel – separate jets and respective entourages required – multiply car emissions by 250 for following paparazzi and police motorcades.

So, beware, America! With Al and Tipper Gore announcing their own marital bliss has ended, we can only expect to see their already massive carbon footprint get even bigger. Really, Al! It would be better for your cause to just stay married, wouldn't it?

THE ANCIENT SOPHISTS

In ancient Greece, there were a group of itinerant intellectuals known as SOPHISTS who taught courses in "excellence" or "virtue," and often utilized rhetoric to achieve their purposes, generally to persuade or convince others. SOPHISTS CLAIMED THAT THEY COULD FIND THE ANSWERS TO ALL QUESTIONS... FOR A PRICE. Some consider the sophists as teachers. Others consider sophists to be the first lawyers. This was the first time in Greece that teachers took fees for teaching. Though not disgraceful in itself, the wise men of Greece prior to that time had never accepted payment for their teaching. The sophists were not, technically speaking, philosophers, but, instead taught any subject for which there was a popular demand. Topics included rhetoric, politics, grammar, etymology, history, physics, and mathematics. The most popular career of a Greek with ability at the time was POLITICS; hence the sophists largely concentrated on teaching rhetoric.

De A. Theuet, Liure II. 83
LIBANIVS LE SOPHISTE
Chap. 31.

The aims of the young politicians whom they trained were to persuade the general public of whatever they wished them to believe. The search for truth was not top priority. Consequently, the sophists undertook to provide a stock of arguments on any subject, or to prove any position. Sophists claimed they had the answers to any argument. THEY BOASTED OF THEIR ABILITY TO MAKE THE WORSE APPEAR THE BETTER, TO PROVE THAT BLACK IS WHITE. Some asserted that it was not necessary to have ANY KNOWLEDGE of a subject to give a satisfactory speech. Thus, sophists ostentatiously answered any question on any subject instantly and without hesitation, and all of this before teleprompters. In this way, the sophists tried to entangle, entrap, and confuse their opponents. They sought also to dazzle by means of strange or flowery metaphors, by unusual figures of speech, by epigrams and paradoxes, and IN GENERAL BY BEING CLEVER AND SMART, RATHER THAN EARNEST AND TRUTHFUL. Hence the definition of the word "sophistry" is using fallacious arguments knowing them to be false. By Aristotle's time, the name "sophist" took on a contemptuous meaning, as he defines "sophist" as "one who reasons falsely for the sake of gain."

MODERN DAY SOPHISTS

Al Gore and his fellow man-made global warming activists are modern day SOPHISTS. They present arguments for the purpose of pushing an agenda and generating dollars both for themselves and for the U.S. government. Think about it. Al Gore doesn't have a degree in climatology. He isn't an expert on greenhouse gases and how they affect global temperatures and the environment. HE IS A POLITICIAN AND A MODERN DAY SOPHIST. As a politician, he is an expert at rhetoric, convincing people that the argument he presents is true and worth supporting, and Al is very good at what he does. Anyone who has seen *An Inconvenient Truth* or heard him speak will attest that Al makes a really strong argument for his cause. The problem is, despite the title of his movie, Al's rhetoric rarely offers truth. This is where RELATIONAL INTELLIGENCE® comes in. EACH OF US AS ACTIVE CITIZENS OF THIS NATION AND THE WORLD NEED TO BE ABLE TO SEPARATE RHETORIC (THE SOPHISTRY) FROM THE REAL TRUTH ABOUT MAN-MADE GLOBAL WARMING.

However, as good as Al is as a sophist, he comes in a distant second. The top spot – the most effective modern day sophist – THAT HONOR GOES TO OUR

PRESIDENT BARACK HUSSEIN OBAMA. Our president and his rhetorical gifts (and with more than a little help from his teleprompters) reigns supreme as the number one modern day sophist. President Obama will arise again in our continued discussions about the man-made global warming hoax. For now, let it simply be said that President Obama, Al Gore and many others in government are the mavens of modern day sophism, and man-made global warming is one of their most impassioned and well-practiced arguments.

Osama Bin Laden Joins Al Gore's Climate Team

The Associated Press reported on January 29, 2010 that Osama Bin Laden released a statement claiming surprising concern for the environment. He stated, "The effects of global warming have touched every continent. Drought and deserts are spreading, while floods and hurricanes unseen before in previous decades have now become frequent."

THE AL QAEDA LEADER BLAMED THE UNITED STATES AND OTHER INDUSTRIALIZED NATIONS FOR CLIMATE CHANGE AND SAID, "THE ONLY WAY TO PREVENT DISASTER WAS TO BREAK THE AMERICAN ECONOMY, CALLING ON THE WORLD TO BOYCOTT U.S. GOODS AND STOP USING THE U.S. DOLLAR. This author is certain that Al Gore will celebrate the addition of Osama Bin Laden to his man-made global warming team.

RQ Insight

When you ask most people how much global warming we are experiencing, they frequently say 10 degrees or more... all within the near future!

The reality is that we are talking about changes within a range of **3 DEGREES CELSIUS... OVER 3,000 YEARS!**

MAN-MADE GLOBAL WARMING

HOAX

part two | THE REAL SCIENCE OF MAN-MADE GLOBAL WARMING

The second part of this book summarizes the strongest, most prevalent scientific data that proves MAN-MADE GLOBAL WARMING IS A HOAX. The following chapters will feature evidence about how the "RECENT" RISE IN GLOBAL TEMPERATURES HAS ABSOLUTELY NOTHING TO DO WITH INCREASES IN HUMAN CARBON DIOXIDE EMISSIONS AND EVERYTHING TO DO WITH NORMAL FLUCTUATIONS IN SOLAR ACTIVITY. We have actually been in a slight cooling period since 1998. Data will also be shared about the true composition of greenhouse gases and how minimal man-made carbon dioxide is to the mix. More importantly, the true nature of carbon dioxide will be revealed; that it is a natural and vital gas that ensures the continuation of life on the planet. The discussion will then move on to other popular man-made global warming myths, including the suggestion that rising global temperatures are killing off polar bears and penguins (when in fact their populations are on the rise), and that hurricanes and tornados are increasing in number and strength (when the only changes scientifically documented show that these storms are actually decreasing in number and are less severe or of the same intensity). Finally, damning evidence will be provided that there is absolutely **NO CONSENUS** among the scientific community in regard to man-made global warming. More and more scientists are coming forth against man-made global warming, and they bring into question why so many overarching and costly policies continued to be supported when the science proves that man-made global warming is, indeed, a HOAX.

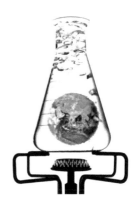

CHAPTER FOUR |

GLOBAL TEMPERATURES:
WHAT ACTUALLY CONSTITUTES WARMING?

First, let me clarify what most people never question. What kind of temperature increases are we talking about when we refer to global warming? THE ANSWER IS A CHANGE OF PLUS 1.2 DEGREES CELSIUS. SINCE 1900, THE AVERAGE SURFACE TEMPERATURE OF THE UNITED STATES HAS ONLY GONE UP BY ONE DEGREE! Given that the average temperature of the Earth has varied within a range of about 3 degrees Celsius during the past 3,000 years, this one degree rise in temperature is well within the norm.

THE REAL SCIENCE OF GLOBAL WARMING

In 2007, three noted scientists, A. B. ROBINSON, N. E. ROBINSON, AND W. SOON, published their article, *Environmental Effects of Increased Atmospheric Carbon Dioxide*. This is currently the most widely reviewed article on this subject and it proves that there is no such thing as man-made global warming.

The Robinsons and Soon begin their argument by clearly showing that the current rise in global temperatures is due to the fact that we are actually recovering from a time known in scientific communities as THE LITTLE ICE AGE. About 300 years ago, around the time George Washington and his army were at Valley Forge, the average temperature of the Earth was about one degree Celsius cooler than it is today. During this time, glaciers in Switzerland and Scandinavia advanced to the point that they forced the abandonment of farms and villages. It was common for rivers in London, St. Petersburg and Moscow to freeze so thoroughly that holding winter fairs on the ice became a local tradition.

When it comes to understanding the truth of why global temperatures are rising, knowing about the Little Ice Age is a big deal! THE TEMPERATURE INCREASE OVER THE LAST 150 YEARS, SO OFTEN CITED AS EVIDENCE OF MAN-MADE GLOBAL WARMING, APPEARS TO BE NOTHING OTHER THAN

Sea Surface Temperatures
Sargasso Sea from 1000 BCE to 2000+ CE

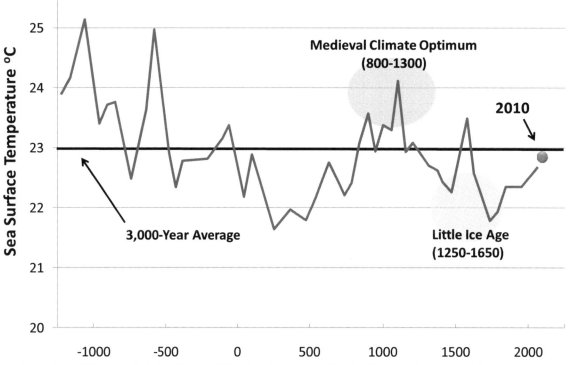

Source: Arthur B. Robinson, Noah E. Robinson and Willie Soon, "Environmental Effects of Increased Atmospheric Carbon Dioxide, Oregon Institute of Science and Medicine, Journal of American Physician and Surgeons (2007), 12, 79-90.
Available at http://www.oism.org/pproject/s33p36.htm

A NATURAL RETURN TO MORE NOMINAL TEMPERATURES AFTER A BIT OF A COLD SNAP **300** TO **400** YEARS AGO. Actually, this return to "normal" is not a smooth line. There are ups and downs along the journey. For example, we have been in a SLIGHT COOLING PERIOD FOR THE LAST **12** YEARS SINCE **1998**! This, of course, comes as a shock to those who see man-made global warming stories in the media every day.

Still, global warming proponents would suggest that even these small increases in temperatures could have devastating effects on our weather patterns, sea levels, etc. But when you consider that back 1,000 years ago, during the Medieval Warm Period, temperatures were one degree Celsius **WARMER** than they are now; their arguments lose validity. BETWEEN THE YEARS **900** AND **1100**, TEMPERATURES ROSE TO LEVELS THE GLOBAL WARMING ACTIVISTS PREDICT FOR **2100**, A PROSPECT THEY INSIST SHOULD BE VIEWED WITH ALARM. HOWEVER, IN EUROPE AT THE TIME, PEOPLE PROSPERED AT THESE TEMPERATURES. The ice in the North Atlantic retreated and permitted Norsemen to colonize Iceland and Greenland (which was actually GREEN at the time). Europe emerged from the Dark Ages and met with bountiful harvests and great economic prosperity. It was so mild that even England and Nova Scotia could grow grapes for wine. Based on the evidence of the Medieval Warming Period, increases in global temperatures are actually nothing to fear. Rather, they are well within planetary norms, and the changes they will bring about are simply a part of nature's ebb and flow.

SOLAR POWER: THE REAL STORY

According to the Robinsons and Soon (and hundreds of other scientists and climatologists), the number one reason global temperatures fluctuate is **SOLAR ACTIVITY**. That's right – THE SUN – not MAN – is what affects global temperature. Only solar activity has any scientific basis for determining rises and falls in global temperatures.

What constitutes solar activity? Well, the sun is not like a light bulb, simply radiating a consistent amount of light and energy. Rather, it is an ever fluctuating 865,000 mile in

Solar Power
Size of a Major Solar Flare Versus Size of Earth

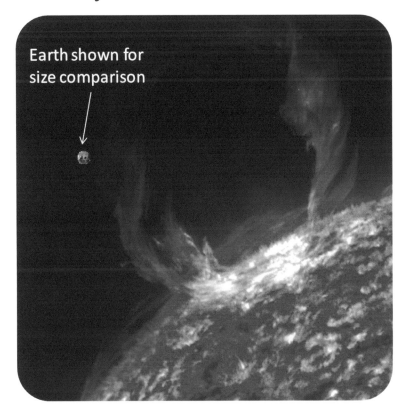

diameter celestial body, so large that it would take about 1,000,000 Earths to make up the same volume as our sun. The constant movement and thermal turbulence emanating from this near perfect sphere causes SOLAR WIND, a supersonic outflow of highly charged particles known as plasma.   As this plasma erupts from the Sun's corona and flies out into interplanetary space, it can knock out power grids on Earth, cause the eerily beautiful aurorae (or northern and southern lights) and SIGNIFICANTLY AFFECTS GLOBAL TEMPERATURES.

As can be seen in the chart below, there is a profound correlation between solar activity and average global temperatures.   As solar activity increases and decreases, so do global temperatures.   Up until 1990, the parallel between solar irradiance and Earth's average temperatures has been uncanny. It is only until recently that the correlations are no longer in sync. Why? Not because of man-made carbon emissions, but rather, man-made science... bad man-made science.

Between 1960 and into the 1980's, scientists were utilizing data from close to **6,000** WEATHER STATIONS to determine global temperatures. By 1990, that number dropped to only 1,500 temperature gathering stations.   MOST OF THE STATIONS LOST WERE FROM COLDER

Global Temperatures and Solar Irradiance
1880 to 2010

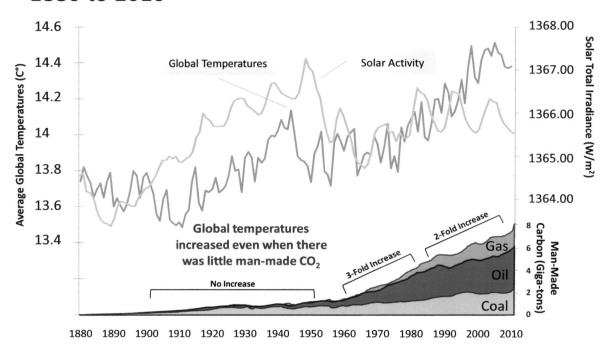

Source: "Arthur B. Robinson, Noah E. Robinson and Willie Soon, "Environmental Effects of Increased Atmospheric Carbon Dioxide, Oregon Institute of Science and Medicine, Journal of American Physician and Surgeons (2007), 12, 79-90.
Available at http://www.oism.org/pproject/s33p36.htm. Updated solar irradiance data available at http://www.leif.org/research/

CLIMATES. According to a 2008 Nongovernmental International Panel on Climate Change (NIPCC) report, *Nature, Not Human Activity, Rules the Climate*, TEMPERATURE DATA HAS NOT BEEN ADJUSTED TO ACCOMMODATE THE LOST STATIONS AND, THEREFORE, GLOBAL TEMPERATURES SHOW FALSE WARMING.

For now, the fact remains that even with the false warming trends currently being reported, temperatures are only increasing because SOLAR ACTIVITY OVER THE LAST 150 YEARS HAS BEEN INCREASING. THERE IS ABSOLUTELY NO EVIDENCE PROVING ANY SIGNIFICANT RELATIONSHIP BETWEEN HUMAN HYDROCARBON USE AND GLOBAL TEMPERATURES. Take a good look at the chart again, especially at the period between 1900 and 1950. During that time, man's contribution to atmospheric CO_2 was extremely limited. YET, DURING THAT TIME, GLOBAL TEMPERATURES WERE ON THE RISE! I repeat again, global temperatures were on the rise even prior to man's expanded use of gas, oil and coal. The reason for this rise is part of a natural cycle of increased solar activity and return to more nominal temperatures after the Little Ice Age.

The assumption that it is man's increased use of hydrocarbons that is causing any rise in global temperatures is misguided and ridiculous. It is true that global temperatures have been rising slightly on average up until 1998. It is also true that this warming trend is coinciding with the human use of coal, oil and natural gas. But, the fact that these two occurrences are happening in tandem DOES NOT MEAN that there is a direct and causal relationship between the two events.

The assumption that human hydrocarbon use and global temperatures have anything to do with one another is an "ILLUSIONARY CORRELATION" (THE ASSUMPTION OF A NON-EXISTENT CORRELATION IN A SET OF DATA THAT FITS ONE'S PRECONCEPTIONS). In other words, it is proof of poor Relational Intelligence®. Scientific, political and environmental circles noted that humans were increasing their use of carbon-based fuels, thereby contributing more carbon dioxide to the atmospheric mix. At the same time, it was also noted that there was a slight warming trend in global temperatures. PRESTO! – the case was made for man-made global warming and the pressure was on to make all data fit this prescribed pattern.

The scientific truth is that it is COINCIDENTAL that global temperatures are rising at the same time as human hydrocarbon use. Solar activity is the only proven driver of global temperatures, and the warming trend we are experiencing is a completely natural and normal event for our planet.

It is hubris to believe that we can affect global temperatures by reducing carbon emissions. Yet, the government remains committed to spending billions of tax dollars to do what is, in

Man-Made Global Warming on Mars?

Planet Earth is not the only planet that has been experiencing a warming trend. According to Habibullo Abdussamatov, head of space research at St. Petersburg Pulkovo astronomical observatory in Russia, Mars, too, appears to be heating up. Data from NASA's Mars Global Surveyor and Odyssey missions reveals that the carbon dioxide "ice caps" near Mars' south pole have been diminishing for three summers in a row.

According to Abdussamatov, "The long-term increases in solar irradiance is heating both the Earth and Mars. Observations of the sun show that as for the increase in temperature, carbon dioxide is 'not guilty,' and as for what lies ahead in the coming decade, it is not catastrophic warming, but a global and very prolonged temperature drop." Abdussamatov suggests that the Earth is entering a prolonged cooling phase because sunspot activity is currently regarded to be "minimal."

His belief is that regardless if man-made emissions of carbon dioxide and other greenhouse gases reach record highs, **GLOBAL TEMPERATURES WILL STILL CONTINUE TO FALL BECAUSE SOLAR ACTIVITY IS DECREASING.**

By the way, the same reduction in sunspot activity coincided with another period in recent history – **THE LITTLE ICE AGE.**

fact, impossible. **THE GLOBAL WARMING ALARMISTS ARE MORE THAN READY TO PUT OUR NATION'S ECONOMIC FUTURE, AS WELL AS THOSE OF MANY OTHER NATIONS, AT RISK IN A FUTILE EFFORT TO REDUCE MANKIND'S MINISCULE CONTRIBUTION OF CO_2 TO THE PLANET, WHICH HAS ABSOLUTELY NO IMPACT ON GLOBAL WARMING IN THE LEAST.**

In summary, the Earth has periods of warming and cooling unrelated to man's activity. The global warming reported by Gore and other warming enthusiasts is actually a return to average temperatures after the Little Ice Age. Finally, the return to "normal" temperature is not a smooth upward line. There are ups and downs. **AS A MATTER OF FACT, WE HAVE BEEN IN A SLIGHT COOLING PERIOD SINCE 1998, AND ACCORDING TO SOME DATA, COULD BE ENTERING A PROFOUND GLOBAL COOLING PERIOD DUE TO DECREASING SOLAR ACTIVITY!**

RQ Insight

Solar activity isn't the only fly in the man-made global warming ointment. Data shows that for the hundred years prior to 1940, sea levels were **RISING** about seven inches per century and glacier lengths were **DECREASING**.

Yet, 84 percent of human annual hydrocarbon use came **AFTER 1940**. More importantly, neither of these trends has accelerated between 1940 and 2007 while **HYDROCARBON USE HAS INCREASED SIX-FOLD!**

CHAPTER FIVE |

GREENHOUSE GASES:
IS CO$_2$ REALLY THE BAD GUY?

There can be no discussion of global warming without the mention of greenhouse gases and the greenhouse effect. Greenhouse gases like carbon dioxide, methane, and nitrous oxide are essential to life on the planet because they trap heat in the Earth's surface troposphere. Without greenhouse gases, the Earth's average temperature would be approximately -18 degrees Celsius (just at zero degrees Fahrenheit). Thanks to the greenhouse effect, average planetary temperatures are a far more balmy 14 degrees Celsius. GREENHOUSE GASES ARE ESSENTIAL TO LIFE ON THIS PLANET. WITHOUT THEM, ALL LIFE ON THE PLANET WOULD BE AT RISK.

The current global warming argument is that through our use of carbon fuels (primarily coal, gas and oil), man-kind is significantly increasing the emission of one greenhouse gas: carbon dioxide (CO$_2$). This excess CO$_2$ is purported to be throwing off the natural balance of greenhouse gases in the atmosphere and putting the planet in danger of warming unnaturally. This phenomenon is called Anthropogenic Global Warming (AGW), but we will just call it man-made global warming. But, what is the truth about carbon dioxide and man's contribution to the levels of this naturally occurring gas? The answer will surprise you.

THE TWO SIDES OF CARBON DIOXIDE (CO$_2$)

Is CO$_2$ a greenhouse gas? Yes, it is! The man-made global warming alarmists have that correct. But from that point on, their arguments begin to fall apart. CO$_2$ IS ACTUALLY A VERY SMALL COMPONENT OF ALL GREENHOUSE GASES. The chart on the next page shows the highly popularized, but HIGHLY MISLEADING, chart of how man-made global warming proponents traditionally depict the role of carbon dioxide levels in the hierarchy of greenhouse gases. Based on this data, carbon dioxide really does appear to be the largest contributing element in greenhouse gas levels. It shows carbon dioxide as **THE** greenhouse gas, surpassing other gases by far in terms of total greenhouse gas make-up.

Greenhouse Gas Concentrations – The Falsehood
Natural and Man-Made Sources Combined

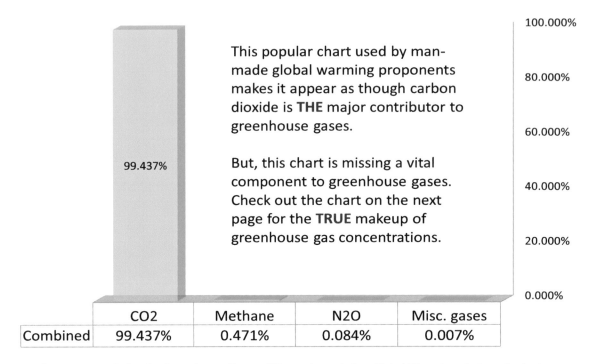

This popular chart used by man-made global warming proponents makes it appear as though carbon dioxide is **THE** major contributor to greenhouse gases.

But, this chart is missing a vital component to greenhouse gases. Check out the chart on the next page for the **TRUE** makeup of greenhouse gas concentrations.

	CO2	Methane	N2O	Misc. gases
Combined	99.437%	0.471%	0.084%	0.007%

Source: "Water Vapor Rules the Greenhouse System." From the website, Global Warming: A closer look at the numbers. Available at http://www.geocraft.com/WVFossils/greenhouse_data.html

It looks like CO_2 makes up 99 percent of all greenhouse gases. What most global warming proponents fail to mention (again and again) is that there is one greenhouse gas missing from their chart. IT'S THE GREENHOUSE GAS CLIMATOLOGISTS, IN THEIR ENTHUSIASTIC FERVOR TO PROVE MAN-MADE GLOBAL WARMING, MAKE IT A POINT TO NEVER MENTION. It is the greenhouse gas that has been swept under the rug in the hopes that the public will never see it come to light. SO, WHAT IS THIS MOST IMPORTANT GREENHOUSE GAS? It is atmospheric WATER VAPOR. Yes, that's right! PLAIN OLD H_2O!

ATMOSPHERIC WATER VAPOR MAKES UP 95 PERCENT OF BOTH PARTICULATE AND VOLUME CONCENTRATION OF GREENHOUSE GASES. Among most climatologists, it is common knowledge that water vapor is indeed the most dominant greenhouse gas, but among man-made global warming enthusiasts, certain governmental groups and news reporters, this fact is under-emphasized, or usually just ignored altogether. Some "scientists" do concede that it might be "A LITTLE MISLEADING" to leave water vapor out, but they nonetheless defend the practice by stating it is "CUSTOMARY" to do so! WHAT!?! Check out the charts on the next two pages and you will see CO_2 in its proper perspective.

Greenhouse Gas Concentrations
The TRUTH

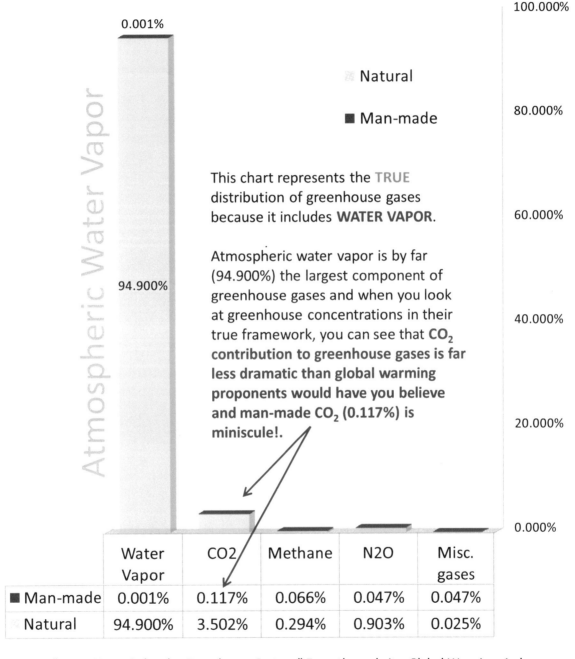

This chart represents the TRUE distribution of greenhouse gases because it includes WATER VAPOR.

Atmospheric water vapor is by far (94.900%) the largest component of greenhouse gases and when you look at greenhouse concentrations in their true framework, you can see that CO_2 contribution to greenhouse gases is far less dramatic than global warming proponents would have you believe and man-made CO_2 (0.117%) is miniscule!.

	Water Vapor	CO2	Methane	N2O	Misc. gases
■ Man-made	0.001%	0.117%	0.066%	0.047%	0.047%
Natural	94.900%	3.502%	0.294%	0.903%	0.025%

Source: "Water Vapor Rules the Greenhouse System." From the website, Global Warming: A closer look at the numbers. Available at http://www.geocraft.com/WVFossils/greenhouse_data.html

Greenhouse Gas Concentrations
And the Truth about Man-Made CO_2

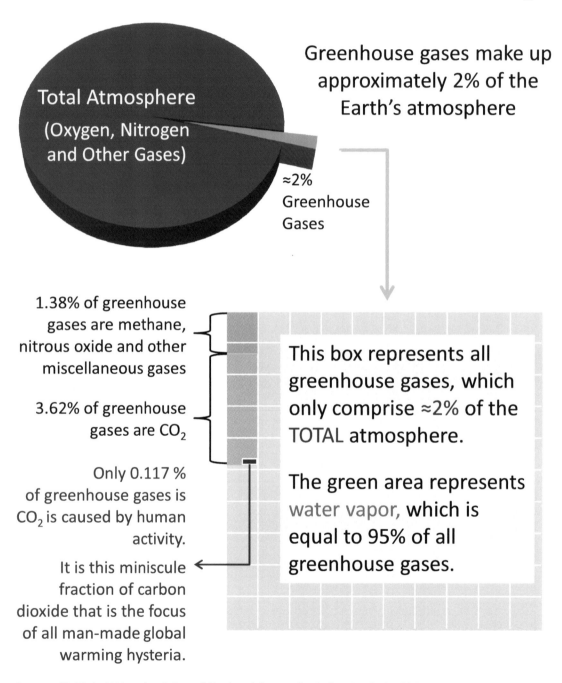

Total Atmosphere
(Oxygen, Nitrogen
and Other Gases)

Greenhouse gases make up approximately 2% of the Earth's atmosphere

≈2%
Greenhouse
Gases

1.38% of greenhouse gases are methane, nitrous oxide and other miscellaneous gases

3.62% of greenhouse gases are CO_2

Only 0.117 % of greenhouse gases is CO_2 is caused by human activity.

It is this miniscule fraction of carbon dioxide that is the focus of all man-made global warming hysteria.

This box represents all greenhouse gases, which only comprise ≈2% of the TOTAL atmosphere.

The green area represents water vapor, which is equal to 95% of all greenhouse gases.

Source: "A Global Warming Primer," National Center for Policy Analysis, 2007.
Available at http://www.ncpa.org/pdfs/GlobalWarmingPrimer.pdf

Let's consider the truth about man's contribution to carbon dioxide as part of the total soup of greenhouse gases. Take a look at the chart on the previous page. Greenhouse gases make up only 2 percent of the Earth's total atmosphere. Of that 2 percent, carbon dioxide represents only 3.62 percent of the greenhouse gases. Now, what would you think is man's contribution to this amount of carbon dioxide?

> MAN-MADE CARBON DIOXIDE IS ONLY 0.117 PERCENT OF THE TOTAL GREENHOUSE GASES, OR 3.23 PERCENT OF THE TOTAL CARBON DIOXIDE IN THE GREENHOUSE GAS MIXTURE.

This is the real hard data. The government's plan to spend trillions of tax-payer dollars to prevent man-made global warming is all focused on reducing the 0.117 percent that man contributes to the total greenhouse gas levels. It's true that there has been a 22 percent increase in CO_2 levels over the last 50 years. It is also true that human consumption of oil, coal and natural gas have contributed to that increase. BUT, HERE IS WHERE OUR GOVERNMENT AND OTHER "MAN-MADE" GLOBAL WARMING PROPONENTS HAVE IT WRONG. THERE IS NO REAL SCIENTIFIC EVIDENCE SUPPORTING THE THEORY THAT THESE RELATIVELY MINOR INCREASES IN CO_2 (0.117 PERCENT) ARE HAVING ANY ENVIRONMENTAL IMPACT AT ALL.

The largest producer of CO_2 on the planet is our oceans. Unless the government's solutions for global warming includes ways to reduce the level of water vapor and carbon dioxide released into the atmosphere by our rivers, lakes and oceans, their impact on greenhouse gas levels will be minimal, if at all. CONSIDER THAT ALL SIX BILLION HUMANS ON THE PLANET PRODUCE A TOTAL OF 8 GIGA-TONS OF CARBON EACH YEAR. COMPARED TO THE 40,000 GIGA-TONS OF CARBON IN THE OCEANS AND BIOSPHERE, MAN-MADE CARBON IS ONLY A VERY MINOR FACTOR IN OVERALL CO_2 LEVELS.

And why does everyone assume increased levels of CO_2 are such a bad thing?

CO_2 IS ACTUALLY VERY BENEFICIAL

No one talks about the benefits of increased carbon dioxide levels. There are three key elements to life: water, oxygen and carbon dioxide. I WILL SAY THAT AGAIN: CARBON DIOXIDE IS ONE OF THE KEY BUILDING BLOCKS OF LIFE. It is not an environmental pollutant as the global warming community would like to suggest. Rather than fearing increased CO_2 levels, it would be more relationally intelligent to consider how this life giving gas enhances life on this planet.

RQ Insight

If water vapor is the major greenhouse gas (approximately 95%), why not tax that instead of CO_2? Simple. Taxing water vapor is like trying to tax the air. CO_2 on the other hand **CAN** be measured (we can quantify how much CO_2 is emitted by man in coal burning power plants, for example).
THEREFORE, CO_2 LENDS ITSELF TO BEING TAXED AND IT HAS THE ADDITIONAL ADVANTAGE OF THE GOVERNMENT INCREASING ITS CONTROL OVER THE ENERGY INDUSTRY.

THINK.

Plants thrive in a rich CO_2 environment. It is their most natural and abundant fertilizer. As more CO_2 is available in the atmosphere, plants grow faster. A 300 PARTS PER MILLION INCREASE IN THE AIR'S CO_2 CONTENT TYPICALLY RAISES THE PRODUCTIVITY OF MOST HERBACEOUS PLANTS BY ABOUT A THIRD. FOR WOODY PLANTS, THE RESPONSE IS EVEN GREATER. Plants are also more drought resistant in CO_2 rich environments, allowing them to grow in drier climates.

Higher CO_2 environments also help offset poor growing conditions like nutrient-poor soil, high soil salinity and low light intensity. As plants grow more quickly and more numerous, they can support an increasing number of animals, including human-kind, in terms of more bountiful food crops. Again, thanks to the work of Drs. Robinson, Soon and others, data has come to light illustrating how OUR SLIGHTLY ELEVATED CO_2 LEVELS ARE ACTUALLY BENEFITTING THE ENVIRONMENT.

Tree ring studies of various species of California, Nevada and Arizona pine show a sharp increase in the growth of these long-lived trees over the last 150 years, corresponding to increases in CO_2 levels. THE U.S. DEPARTMENT OF AGRICULTURE REPORTS THAT U.S. FORESTS HAVE INCREASED 40 PERCENT IN THE LAST 50 YEARS. THERE IS ALSO EVIDENCE SHOWING THAT, THANKS TO INCREASED CO_2 LEVELS, THE AMAZONIAN RAIN FORESTS ARE GAINING TWO TONS OF BIOMASS PER ACRE EACH YEAR!

Carbon dioxide is a natural part of our environment. Yes, human use of hydrocarbons has increased atmospheric carbon dioxide levels slightly over the last 150 years. However, the amount is insignificant next to the carbon dioxide released by our oceans, and has no impact on our global temperatures, which are ruled by solar activity. In addition, increased carbon dioxide is of benefit to all plant species, making them grow more quickly and abundantly. The threat of carbon dioxide emissions so feared by man-made global warming proponents is totally unfounded.

Cure World Hunger Through Increased CO$_2$

Harrison Brown, a geochemist who supervised the production of plutonium for the Manhattan Project, wrote in his 1954 book titled, **The Challenge of Man's Future**, that the production of the food needed to feed an increasing world population could be advances by human-manipulated greenhouse effects, including the forced introduction of CO$_2$ into the atmosphere.

Lamenting that "the earth's atmosphere contains only a minute concentration – about 0.03 percent" of carbon dioxide, Brown observed that, "It has been demonstrated that a tripling of carbon dioxide concentration in the air will approximately double the growth rates of tomatoes, alfalfa, and sugar beets, etc.."

Brown then argued on that "controlled atmospheres enriched in carbon dioxide" would be an essential component of enormous greenhouses built to house plants in the nutrient-rich solutions. Brown realized these huge greenhouses would be very costly. His conclusion? Pump more carbon dioxide into the atmosphere in all regions of the world!

"If, in some manner, the carbon dioxide content of the atmosphere could be increased threefold, world food production might be doubled." Brown was

clear that **WORLD GOVERNMENTS SHOULD COOPERATE TO GENERATE EXCESS CO$_2$, NOT TO REDUCE HUMAN-GENERATED CARBON DIOXIDE FROM THE ATMOSPHERE.**

Brown went so far as to recommend burning more coal to generate electricity, precisely because burning coal emitted carbon dioxide. "There are between 18 and 20 tons of carbon dioxide over every acre of the earth's surface," he noted. "In order to double the amount of CO$_2$ in the atmosphere, at least 500 billion tons of coal would have to be burned – an amount six times greater than that which has been consumed during all of human history."

Again, let's look at a quick summary of THE **REAL** INCONVENIENT TRUTH OF MAN-MADE CO$_2$:

FIRST: Water vapor (not carbon dioxide) equals 95 percent of all greenhouse gases. REMEMBER THAT GREENHOUSE GASES ONLY EQUAL ABOUT 2 PERCENT OF THE TOTAL ATMOSPHERE.

SECOND: Carbon dioxide only makes up 3.62 percent of all greenhouse gases. Of that total, only 3.23 percent is produced by mankind, or **0.117** PERCENT OF THE TOTAL OF GREENHOUSE GASES. AGAIN THIS **0.117** PERCENT IS THE REASON THE GOVERNMENT PLANS TO LEGISLATE CARBON EMISSIONS.

THIRD: Finally, do the math. Our government is willing to invest trillions of dollars, and tax trillions of dollars, to offset the 0.117 percent of carbon dioxide that human-kind produces, which, in reality, doesn't influence global temperatures or climate in the least! THIS IS ABSOLUTELY LAUGHABLE… IF IT DID NOT HAVE SUCH DIRE FINANCIAL CONSEQUENCES.

Carbon Dioxide, Correlation, Causation and Relational Intelligence®

Cum hoc ergo propter hoc is Latin for "with this, therefore because of this." Stated more clearly, it means that since one thing and another occur simultaneously, then one must cause the other. Man-made global warming is one of the biggest examples of *cum hoc ergo propter hoc* or "coincidental correlation."

The major assumption of those in the man-made global warming camp is that because the human-caused carbon dioxide levels have increased at a time when global temperatures are also increasing, *cum hoc ergo propter hoc*, man must be causing global warming. This is a complete fallacy. It is in fact coincidental that global temperatures are rising during the time that man has been making use of carbon-based fuels. There is a difference between correlation and causation. Just because both CO_2 levels and temperatures are rising at the same time **DOES NOT** mean that one causes the other. Yet, in a stunning lack of Relational Intelligence®, man-made global warming proponents insist it does.

Let us take a moment to consider the three basic assumptions that separate correlation and causation and see how they differ.

Assumption that X causes Y

In true causation, X causes Y. For instance, fire causes smoke. Except in specific circumstances, this statement is one of true causation. However, many statements can be made that initially appear to be causation that are actually mere correlations. For instance, it has been scientifically proven that you can estimate the chirp rate of a cricket from the temperature in Fahrenheit using the formula (chirps = 3.777 * degrees – 137.22) with r-0.9919 accuracy. However, nobody – except perhaps Al Gore – would actually believe that crickets cause temperature changes.

Assumption that if X causes Y then Y causes X

Just because X causes Y, it doesn't mean that the opposite is true. For instance, smoke does not **CAUSE** fire. Consider the following statements to see how strong causations do not mean that the reverse is true.

- Cutting people is a crime. Surgeons cut people. Therefore, surgeons are criminals.
- If it rains, the ground gets wet. The ground is wet. Therefore, it rained.
- If you drop a hammer on your foot, your foot will hurt. Your foot hurts. Therefore, you dropped a hammer on it.

The assumptions become significantly more dangerous when combining two or more causations into a new statement.

○ More cows die in India in the summer months. More ice cream is consumed in the summer months. Therefore, the consumption of ice cream in the summer months is killing Indian cows.

ASSUMPTION THAT MANIPULATING Y COULD ACTUALLY AFFECT X

It is when people take a causation statement and try to reverse the causality that we move into the realm of logical fallacy. For instance, during World War II, American supply planes in the Pacific theater would drop cargo via parachute on primitive islands where the United States and Japan had military bases. Islanders who found these cargo packages went from the Stone Age to the 20th century overnight. All of the sudden, they had access to medicines, canned food, canvas tents, steel tools and sometimes even weapons. Not only were the islanders impressed by the cargo, but also how it was being delivered to them… literally falling from the sky. LOCAL RELIGIONS BEGAN TO EMERGE DESIGNED TO ENCOURAGE THE "SKY-GODS" TO OFFER UP MORE BOUNTY FROM THE HEAVENS.

Imitating the western foreigners, islanders carved wooden representations of the headphones they saw the soldiers wearing so that they too could talk to the "sky-god" planes. They learned to wave landing signal flags and even light signal fires which would sometimes trick an off-course supply plane to make a drop. THIS BEHAVIOR IS CALLED "SYMPATHETIC MAGIC" AND APPEARS IN OTHER CULTURES. PEOPLE MIMIC THE EFFECT TO GET THE CAUSE. When the war ended and the airbases were abandoned, the "sky-gods" stopped their offerings and the islanders had to go back to their original beliefs. YET, EVEN TODAY, THE JON FRUM "CARGO CULT" IS STILL ACTIVE ON THE ISLAND OF TANNA, VANUATU. However, even the Jon Frum believers can be more easily understood than those who are members of the man-made global warming cult.

DESPITE THE FACT **that recent increases in global temperatures are due to solar and cloud activity and the cyclical upswing from the Little Ice Age…**

DESPITE THE FACT **that man's contribution to carbon dioxide levels in the atmosphere are so small as to be absolutely non-relevant…**

DESPITE THE FACT **that so many of the catastrophic predictions made by man-made global warming enthusiasts have failed to materialize…**

THE FALLACY OF MAN-MADE GLOBAL WARMING PERSISTS BASED ON A SIMPLE CORRELATION. TEMPERATURES APPEAR TO HAVE RISEN AT THE SAME TIME AS MAN HAS BEEN BURNING FOSSIL FUELS.

This is correlation, NOT causation. And the further fallacy that man can actually flip the correlation and affect global temperatures by decreasing the miniscule amount of carbon dioxide we produce is even more ridiculous! The most telling fact perhaps is that since 1998, we have actually been in a slight cooling period.

Delusions of Grandeur

It is folly for man to think that he has control over the planet. Consider the following story. On February 3rd, 1995, actor Charlton Heston came onto Rush Limbaugh's radio show to read an excerpt from the prologue of Michael Crichton's book, Jurassic Park. Below is a copy of the text he read.

You think man can destroy the planet? What intoxicating vanity. Let me tell you about our planet. Earth is four-and-a-half-billion-years-old. There's been life on it for nearly that long: 3.8 billion years. Bacteria first; later the first multicellular life, then the first complex creatures in the sea, on the land. Then finally the great sweeping ages of animals, the amphibians, the dinosaurs, at last the mammals, each one enduring millions on millions of years, great dynasties of creatures rising, flourishing, dying away -- all this against a background of continuous and violent upheaval. Mountain ranges thrust up, eroded away, cometary impacts, volcano eruptions, oceans rising and falling, whole continents moving, an endless, constant, violent change, colliding, buckling to make mountains over millions of years. Earth has survived everything in its time. It will certainly survive us. If all the nuclear weapons in the world went off at once and all the plants, all the animals died and the earth was sizzling hot for a hundred thousand years, life would survive, somewhere: under the soil, frozen in Arctic ice. Sooner or later, when the planet was no longer inhospitable, life would spread again. The evolutionary process would begin again. It might take a few billion years for life to regain its present variety. Of course, it would be very different from what it is now, but the earth would survive our folly, only we would not.

If the ozone layer gets thinner, ultraviolet radiation sears the earth, so what? Ultraviolet radiation is good for life It's powerful energy. It promotes mutation, change. Many forms of life will thrive with more UV radiation. Many others will die out. Do you think this is the first time that's happened? Think about oxygen. Necessary for life now, but oxygen is actually a metabolic poison, a corrosive gas, like fluorine. When oxygen was first produced as a waste product by certain plant cells some three billion years ago, it created a crisis for all other life on earth. Those plants were polluting the environment, exhaling a lethal gas. Earth eventually had an atmosphere incompatible with life. Nevertheless, life on earth took care of itself. In the thinking of the human being a hundred years is a long time. A hundred years ago we didn't have cars, airplanes, computers or vaccines. It was a whole different world, but to the earth, a hundred years is nothing. A million years is nothing. This planet lives and breathes on a much vaster scale. We can't imagine its slow and powerful rhythms, and we haven't got the humility to try. We've been residents here for the blink of an eye. If we're gone tomorrow, the earth will not miss us.

It is the vanity of man to believe that everything revolves around him and therefore can be affected by him. It is a delusion of grandeur to believe that any effort we make will actually change the temperature of the Earth. The only thing we can do on a rainy day is carry an umbrella. When it comes to the climate and the natural forces of the planet, human kind simply isn't capable of making any real impact.

RQ Insight

"It ain't what you don't know that gets you into trouble.

IT'S WHAT YOU KNOW FOR SURE THAT JUST AIN'T SO."

– Mark Twain

CHAPTER SIX |
MORE INCONVENIENT TRUTHS

HURRICANES AND TORNADOS

Another favorite claim made by man-made global warming proponents is that even minor changes in global temperatures will lead to potentially catastrophic changes in our weather patterns. Let's check the data on two of the most devastating weather occurrences we face in the United States today: hurricanes and tornados.

Being a Florida resident, this author can speak with some level of credibility about hurricanes. They are extremely powerful storms that demand respect and caution, as was demonstrated by the extreme devastation caused by Hurricane Katrina. However, again with the help of the "Calamity Jane" media, fear of these storms is being leveraged to create more fuel for the man-made global warming fire. It is said that global warming will call for stronger and far more numerous storms. The fact is, since 1900, the number of Atlantic hurricanes that have made landfall has remained stable. THERE HAS BEEN NO INCREASE IN THE NUMBER OF STORMS FOR THE LAST 100 YEARS! The same can be said for the intensity of storms. THERE HAS BEEN NO INCREASE IN MAXIMUM HURRICANE WIND SPEED FOR THE LAST 60 YEARS. What has happened is that more and more of our population in the U.S. has made the choice to build homes closer and closer to the ocean. So while property damage from hurricanes has increased, the intensity of hurricanes has not.

In late 2008, weather forecasters predicted an extremely busy hurricane season for 2009. As it turned out, very few hurricanes developed, much less gained any strength before making landfall. Faces still red from their "crystal-ball" forecasts the year before, undaunted forecasters continue to make their predictions and forecasts frequently based on computer models. These predictions are just like many of the predictions made about man-made global warming... based on computer-models that are yet nowhere accurate enough to do more than be a scientist's version of a video game.

Moving on to TORNADOS, again the data suggests that we have nothing to fear from the current slight and completely natural increase in global temperatures. SINCE 1950, THE

NUMBER OF SEVERE TORNADOS IN THE UNITED STATES HAS BEEN DECREASING. During this period, world hydrocarbon use INCREASED six-fold while violent tornado frequency DECREASED by 43 percent.

POLAR BEARS & PENGUINS: THE CANARIES FOR GLOBAL WARMING CULTISTS

You may have heard of the practice used by miners up until as recently as 1987 in some mines. CANARIES were once regularly used in coal mining as an early warning system. Life for an actual canary in a coal mine could be short but very meaningful to coal miners. Early coal mines did not have ventilation systems, so miners would routinely bring caged canaries into new coal seams. Canaries are especially sensitive to methane and carbon monoxide, which made them ideal for detecting any dangerous gas build-ups. As long as the canaries in the coal mine kept singing, the miners knew their air supply was safe. A DEAD CANARY IN A COAL MINE SIGNALED THE NEED FOR IMMEDIATE EVACUATION.

Today, those who claim global warming is a major concern threatening human-kind cite the deaths of polar bears and penguins. The argument set forth by Al Gore in his book and later in his movie says that polar bears and penguins are rapidly dying due to man-made global warming, and soon we will only see polar bears and penguins in zoos. Then, Gore and others lead us to believe that with a 20-foot increase in sea levels, violent hurricanes and tornados, and inability to grow food, mankind will suffer the fate of the polar bears and penguins.

POLAR BEARS THRIVING IN WARMER CLIMATES

Today, those who claim global warming is a major concern threatening human-kind cite a major decrease in the polar bear and penguin populations. Polar bears and penguins have become the "canaries" for the man-made global warming movement. Their disappearance is the harbinger of the threat to our own existence. The image that has become synonymous with threat of climate change is one of a lone polar bear seemingly lost among rapidly disappearing ice floes. Al Gore tells us that polar bears are starting to drown in significant numbers as their ice pack territories melt away.

However, recent research by the Polar Specialist Group of the World Conservation Union presents a very different picture. They report that of **20** distinct subpopulations of bears, only one or possibly two subpopulations in Baffin Bay are declining. More than half of these subpopulations were stable and two others were actually increasing around the Beaufort Sea.

RQ Insight

Remember "Shark Syndrome Perception?" Polar bears and penguins stir our emotions and cause us to believe in man-made global warming far more than scientific evidence warrants.

∟ THINK.

EVEN MORE DAMNING FOR GLOBAL WARMING CULTISTS IS THAT THE TERRITORIES WHERE POLAR BEAR SUBPOPULATIONS HAVE BEEN IN DECLINE ARE ACTUALLY GETTING COLDER OVER THE PAST 50 YEARS.

"There aren't just a few more bears. There are a **HELL** of a lot more bears."

Mitch Taylor
The Telegraph
Canadian Scientist who has studied polar bears up close for more than 20 years. *(emphasis added)*

THE AREAS WHERE POLAR BEARS ARE STABLE AND/OR FLOURISHING ARE GETTING WARMER!

Recent tallies show that total polar bear population has actually increased dramatically from about **5,000 POLAR BEARS** in the 1960's to **25,000 TODAY!** Al Gore's statement about "drowning polar bears" came shortly after a single sighting of four dead bears after "an abrupt windstorm" in an area of one of the increasing polar bear populations.

If one really wanted to save the polar bears, working to "stop" global warming by several magnitudes isn't the most effective strategy. **EVERY YEAR 300 TO 500 POLAR BEARS ARE SHOT BY HUNTERS!** Compared to the numbers global warming proponents say are drowning each year (four is the number provided by the ever unreliable Al Gore), we could easily save many more bears if we simply imposed stricter hunting restrictions.

The Polar Bear Population Growth

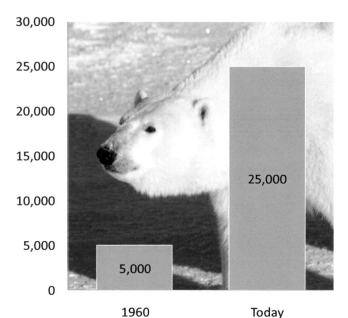

Polar bear numbers increased dramatically from around 5,000 in the 1960s to as many as 25,000 today, higher than at any time in the 20th century.

Of the distinct polar bear populations worldwide, only two populations are decreasing. The majority of the populations are stable or increasing.

Source: Stefan Norris, Lynn Rosentrater and Pal Martin Eid, "Polar Bears at Risk: A WWF Status Report, "World Wildlife Fund, May 2002.
Available at http://www.wwf.org.uk/filelibrary/pdf/polar_bears_at_risk_report.pdf

HOW DO THESE THINGS GET STARTED?

If you are not familiar with the photo below, it is of a polar bear mother and cub seemingly stranded on a melting ice flow adrift at sea. This particular image is iconic to the man-made global warming cause. It illustrates how, thanks to man's mythical contribution to global warming, we are dooming the majestic (not to mention, cute) polar bears, along with many other species to hardship, famine and ultimately slow, painful extinction.

Environment Canada, whose mandate is to preserve and enhance the quality of Canada's natural environment, distributed this photo to several media agencies, including the Associated Press. From AP, the photo began to make its way to media outlets across the globe. Captions like the following from *Daily Mail* began appearing everywhere.

> *"They cling precariously to the top of what is left of the ice floe, their fragile grip the perfect symbol of the tragedy of global warming."*

The photo even made it to the front page of the New York Times. At some point, Al Gore got his hands on the photo and began to feature it in his presentations. With the image blown up to movie theater proportions behind him, Gore would play on his audience sympathies by stating:

67

"Their habitat is melting... beautiful animals, literally being forced off the planet. They are in trouble, got nowhere else to go."

SO SWAYED BY THE WORDS AND THE IMAGE, AUDIENCE MEMBERS NEVER BOTHER TO QUESTION THE ACTUAL ORIGIN OF THIS IMAGE (ANOTHER SIGN OF POOR RELATIONAL INTELLIGENCE®.) They simply assume that this mother bear and cub have met their tragic end soon after the picture was taken, and are drawn deeper into the man-made global warming rhetoric. The problem is, the inconvenient truth has come out and the propaganda surrounding the photo was revealed.

You see, the photo was taken by an Australian graduate student by the name of Amanda Byrd while she was on a University of Alaska Fairbanks field trip. A marine biology major, Amanda snapped the image while on board ship and then downloaded the photos to a ship's computer. At that point, a shipmate, Dan Crosbie, found the image and sent it along to the Canadian Ice Service. The Canadian Ice Service sent the photo to Environment Canada and the man-made global warming propaganda machine took over from there.

When the truth of the photo's origins became public, Amanda Byrd was interviewed about the photo that she never realized was going to be posted anywhere other than her personal photo album. SHE EXPLAINED THAT THE PHOTO WAS TAKEN DURING THE ARCTIC SUMMER OF 2004, SO IT WAS NOT SURPRISING THAT THE ICE WAS MELTING. The bears didn't appear to be in "danger" and were "healthy, fat and seemingly comfortable on the ice berg." There were other larger ice floes nearby and they were not that far from shore. BY THE WAY, POLAR BEARS CAN SWIM UP TO 60 MILES A DAY AND ARE SUPREMELY AT HOME IN THE WATER.

Poor Amanda never intended or designed to have her simple snapshot stolen for the man-made global warming propaganda cause. But, as you will see, there is little that warming proponents wouldn't do to further their cause.

PENGUIN EMPIRES

The story is similar for penguins. The 2005 documentary, ***March of the Penguins***, featured a colony of Emperor Penguins that make their home five hundred yards from the French research station, Dumont d'Urville. This particular penguin colony has been constantly monitored since 1952, and its population was stable at about six thousand breeding pairs, until the 1970s, when it dropped suddenly to about three thousand pairs. Biologists are yet uncertain why the number dropped but, since the numbers have been stable again for the last 30+ years, climate change seems an unlikely cause. More importantly, this colony is only one of more than about **40** colonies in Antarctica, and it is a small colony at that. Larger colonies of more than **20,000** pairs exist and their numbers appear to be stable and/or increasing. According to the International Union for Conservation of Nature and Natural Resource (IUCN), they have placed Emperor Penguins in their category of least concern, meaning that this species did not qualify for critically endangered, endangered, vulnerable or near threatened categories. In other words, there is a healthy and abundant population of Emperor Penguins in the world.

The only reason the March of the Penguins colony is so heavily cited in penguin studies is their proximity to the French research station. In fact, Emperor Penguins are not even the dominant penguin species in Antarctica. The Adélie penguins are and in the past **20** years, their populations have increased more than **40** percent. It is just one more example of how man-made global warming alarmists aren't giving us the full story.

CHAPTER SEVEN |
THE UTTER LACK OF CONSENSUS SCIENCE

Just before his departure to the United Nations Climate Change Conference in Copenhagen, Denmark in December of 2009, President Obama stated "THE SCIENCE REQUIRES US TO TAKE ACTION IN COPENHAGEN." Not so fast! There is plenty of science and scientists that do not push us to take action, despite what President Obama says. IN FACT, IT IS DOUBTFUL THERE WAS EVER ANY CONSENSUS AMONG SCIENTISTS IN REGARD TO MAN-MADE GLOBAL WARMING.

Our government, many university scientists, and especially Al Gore, like to talk about "consensus science," (i.e., "most scientists agree that our reliance on fossil fuels is causing a detrimental increase in carbon emissions leading to man-made global warming"). THE PROBLEM IS THAT SCIENCE IS THE LAST PLACE YOU WANT TO START LOOKING FOR CONSENSUS. Science is usually a field of study free of subjectivity, and that relies on repeated unbiased testing and experimentation to come up with results. SCIENTISTS AS A NORM CHALLENGE EACH OTHER'S ASSUMPTIONS AND SEEK ALTERNATIVE HYPOTHESES TO TEST. In science, if not anywhere else, we as a species distinguish ourselves through our willingness to constantly question how we understand the world around us and how we relate to it.

Michael Crichton (best known for his novels, but also a graduate of Harvard Medical School and a former postdoctoral fellow at the Salk Institute for Biological Studies) warned his audience of the dangers of "consensus science" in a 2003 speech.

> *Historically, the claim of consensus has been the first refuge of scoundrels; it is a way to avoid debate by claiming that the matter is already settled. Whenever you hear the consensus of scientists agrees on something or other, reach for your wallet, because you're being had. Let's be clear: the work of science has nothing whatever to do with consensus.*

AL GORE VERSUS REAL SCIENTISTS!

[Global warming is] the worst scandal in history… When people come to know what the truth is, they will feel deceived by science and scientists.
Dr. Kiminori Itoh, UN IPCC scientist
award-winning PhD environmental physical chemist

I am convinced that the current alarm over carbon dioxide is mistaken… Fears about man-made global warming are unwarranted and are not based on good science.
Dr. Will Happer, Award Winning Physicist
Professor at the department of physics at Princeton University and Former Director of Energy Research at the Department of Energy

Gore prompted me to start delving into the science again and I quickly found myself solidly in the skeptic camp. Climate models can at best be useful for explaining climate changes after the fact.
Hajo Smit, Meteorologist from Holland
Former member of the Dutch UN IPCC committee

The scientists are virtually screaming from the rooftops now. THE DEBATE IS OVER! There's no longer any debate in the scientific community about this.
Al Gore
former "next President of the United States"

Many [scientists] are now searching for a way to back out quietly (from promoting warming fears), without having their professional careers ruined.
James A. Peden, Atmospheric physicist
Formerly of the Space Research & Coordination Center in Pittsburgh

The 'global warming scare' is being used as a political tool to increase government control over American lives, incomes and decision making. It has no place in Society's activities.
Jack Schmitt, Award-wining Astronaut/Geologist
Moonwalker who flew on the Apollo 17 mission

I have yet to see credible proof of carbon dioxide driving climate change, yet alone man-made CO_2 driving it. The atmospheric hot-spot is missing and the ice core data refute this. When will we collectively awake from this deceptive delusion?
Dr. G. LeBlanc Smith, retired Principal Research Scientist with Australia's CSIRO

Consensus is the business of politics. Science, on the contrary, requires only one investigator who happens to be right, which means that he or she has results that are verifiable by reference to the real world. In science consensus is irrelevant. What is relevant is reproducible results. The greatest scientists in history are great precisely because they broke with the consensus.

THE FACT IS, WHEN IT COMES TO MAN-MADE GLOBAL WARMING, THERE IS NO CONSENSUS AMONG THE SCIENTIFIC COMMUNITY, DESPITE THE GOVERNMENT'S AND AL GORE'S INSISTENCE THERE IS. Bolstered by grant and other research monies, there are enclaves of scientists pushing the man-made global warming agenda, but they are not without challengers, which the media usually choose to ignore.

BUT, THERE IS A GROWING NUMBER WITHIN THE SCIENTIFIC COMMUNITY WHO ARE WILLING TO BREAK THE MOLD AND COME FORWARD WITH THE TRUTH ABOUT THE CURRENT WARMING TRENDS WE ARE EXPERIENCING... THAT THEY ARE PART OF A NATURAL TEMPERATURE CYCLE THAT THE EARTH HAS BEEN MOVING THROUGH FOR THOUSANDS OF YEARS. The data is out there if people are willing to look at it. However, the government, universities and the media help to keep these voices of opposition at bay.

THE INFAMOUS HOCKEY STICK HOAX

In the IPCC Second Assessment *Summary for Policymakers* in 1996, a diagram showing the past 1,000 years of Earth temperatures from tree rings, ice cores and thermometers showed the Medieval Warming, the Little Age and the slight warming we are having since the late 20th century. Although some argued about mixing temperature data from different sources (tree rings, ice cores with thermometer measurements, and all the limitations of these measurements), the diagram had strong validity with historical weather records.

Five years later in 2001, the IPCC's Climate Change Report presented a totally different diagram for the past 1,000 years of Earth temperatures. THE MEDIEVAL WARMING AND THE LITTLE ICE AGE HAD BEEN EXPUNGED FROM HISTORY and a significant warming from 1910 on was the highlight of the diagram. The diagram which looked like a hockey stick, had a great visual impact and implied was that the "runaway" temperature rise in the 20th Century was due to human industrialization.

THIS "HOCKEY STICK" DIAGRAM DERIVED FROM A 1998 STUDY BY MICHAEL MANN AND HIS COLLEAGUES. Mann was a recently minted Ph.D. and this study brought him fame, fortune and great prestige because it basically provided the foundation for the man-made global warming to be perpetuated. At an early age, he became editor of a major scientific journal

Hockey Stick Data Manipulation

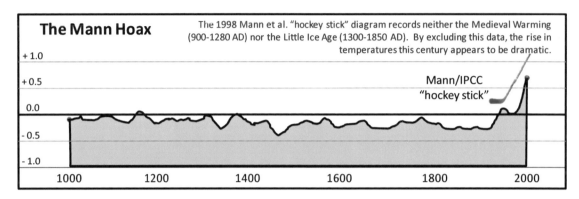

The Mann Hoax

The 1998 Mann et al. "hockey stick" diagram records neither the Medieval Warming (900-1280 AD) nor the Little Ice Age (1300-1850 AD). By excluding this data, the rise in temperatures this century appears to be dramatic.

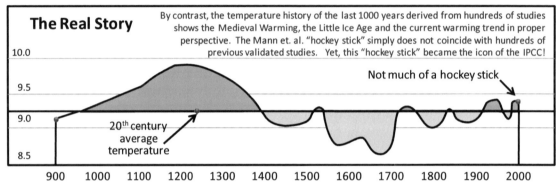

The Real Story

By contrast, the temperature history of the last 1000 years derived from hundreds of studies shows the Medieval Warming, the Little Ice Age and the current warming trend in proper perspective. The Mann et. al. "hockey stick" simply does not coincide with hundreds of previous validated studies. Yet, this "hockey stick" became the icon of the IPCC!

Source: McIntyre, S. and McKitrick, R. 2003; Corrections to the Mann et al "Proxy data base and Northern Hemisphere temperature service, 1998. Energy and Environment 14: 751-771.

and became an IPCC lead author. Mann was a hero, and was besieged by the media. But, where and how did Mann get the data for his infamous hockey chart? He mainly used tree ring data as a temperature proxy. This assumes that in warmer times, trees grow more vigorously than in colder times. To this were added thermometer measurements, mainly from urban areas, to cover the period after 1908.

THE EXPUNGING OF THE MEDIEVAL WARMING AND THE LITTLE ICE AGE WAS CONTRARY TO THOUSANDS OF HISTORICAL RECORDS AND SCIENTIFIC STUDIES, YET THESE WERE REDUCED TO INSIGNIFICANCE IN THE MANN STUDY. The IPCC Climate Change 2001 Report (Section 2.3.3 "Was there a 'Little Ice Age' and 'Medieval Warm Period'?") restricted the Medieval Warming and the Little Ice Age to very slight changes that occurred only in the North Atlantic region, and suggested that they were due to slightly altered patterns of atmospheric circulation.

THE IPCC UNCRITICALLY ACCEPTED THE "HOCKEY STICK" AND REJECTED, WITHOUT EXPLANATION, THE THOUSANDS OF SCIENTIFIC STUDIES BY REPUTABLE SCIENTISTS OF MEDIEVAL WARMING AND THE

LITTLE ICE AGE. The Medieval Warming had been dismissed. It was a nuisance. The impact of the Little Ice Age was greatly diminished and was attributed to "constricted" global circulation. However, this finding offers absolutely no comfort to the millions of people who died of cold or cold-induced famine in the Little Ice Age. USING MANN'S DATA ALONE, THE IPCC THEN CLAIMED THAT THERE WAS UNPRECEDENTED WARMING IN THE 20TH CENTURY. THE "HOCKEY STICK" PROVED IT. THE IPCC USED THE "HOCKEY STICK" ON THE FIRST PAGE OF THE SUMMARY FOR POLICYMAKERS AND DISPLAYED IT FOUR MORE TIMES, IN SOME PLACES OCCUPYING HALF A PAGE. Clearly the IPCC endorsed the "hockey stick." In 2000, Mann's "hockey stick" was featured in a U.S. government report.

Science methodology is such that new data and resulting conclusions are critically analyzed, repeated, refined or rejected. This "hockey stick" graphic was in contrast to conclusions derived from thousands of studies using boreholes in ice, lakes, rivers and oceans, glacial deposits, flood deposits, sea level data, soils, volcanoes, windblown sand, isotopes, pollen, peat, fossils, cave deposits, agriculture and contemporary records. When extraordinary conclusions are made, there needs to be extraordinary data in support. This is exactly what happened with the Mann study. IT WAS DEMOLISHED ON THE BASIS OF REAL SCIENCE.

REAL SCIENTISTS STEP UP

Two Canadians, Steven McIntyre and Ross McKitrick, requested the original data from Mann that underpinned his study. This was like extracting teeth. After much bluster, stonewalling and hiding behind the veil of confidentiality, the data was provided in dribs and drabs. The original data set provided for validation and repeatability, a normal process of science, was incomplete. BECAUSE U.S. FEDERAL FUNDS HAD BEEN USED TO SUPPORT MANN'S STUDY, BY LAW THE DATA HAD TO BE MADE AVAILABLE. As for how the Mann paper ended up being published in the journal, *Nature*, it seemed clear that NO REVIEWER OF THE MANN ET AL. PAPER IN NATURE HAD REQUESTED THE ORIGINAL DATA UPON WHICH THE PAPER WAS BASED. If they had, *Nature* would not have published a paper using such incomplete data. This is not the place to speculate on whether this was a lapse in editorial standards or whether *Nature* had another agenda. However, extraordinary conclusions and the dismissal of thousands of previous scientific studies on the Medieval Warming and Little Ice Age should have stimulated

Michael Mann and his infamous tree rings

reviewers and editors of **Nature** to view the primary data and calculations as a normal part of scientific due diligence.

MCINTYRE AND MCKITRICK FOUND THAT THE MANN DATA DID NOT PRODUCE THE CLAIMED RESULTS DUE TO COLLATION ERRORS, UNJUSTIFIABLE TRUNCATION OF EXTRAPOLATION OF SOURCE DATA, OBSOLETE DATA, GEOGRAPHICAL LOCATION ERRORS, INCORRECT CALCULATION OF PRINCIPAL COMPONENTS AND OTHER QUALITY CONTROL DEFECTS.

The IPCC used the Mann diagram in 2001 as the central tool to show that man-made global warming started in the 20th Century. It is clear that MANN'S DATA USED TO CONSTRUCT THE "HOCKEY STICK" WAS MEANINGLESS, THAT ADEQUATE DUE DILIGENCE WAS NOT UNDERTAKEN BY THE AUTHORS, REVIEWERS OR THE EDITORS!

Using Mann's own data, McIntyre and McKitrick SHOWED THAT THE WARMING IN THE EARLY 15TH CENTURY EXCEEDS ANY WARMING OF THE 20TH CENTURY. McIntyre and McKitrick showed that the Mann study gave great weight to the 20th Century tree ring data from the Sierra Nevada Mountains of California. This data was collected by others and was not compared with thermometer measurements that existed for that area, but was compared with thermometer measurements from urban areas. The trees used were ancient, slow-growing, high-altitude bristlecone pine trees. Such trees can live up to 5,000 years, hence are ideal for climate studies. The trees showed a growth spurt after 1910. The research on the bristlecone trees was used by Mann to show that temperature started to increase in 1910. HOWEVER, THE ORIGINAL PAPER USED BY MANN NOT ONLY DEMONSTRATED THAT THE TREE RING TEMPERATURE PROXY MUST BE USED WITH CAUTION, BUT ALSO THAT THE BRISTLECONE TREE RING DATA SHOWING A POST-1910 GROWTH SPURT COULD NOT BE EXPLAINED BY LOCAL OR REGIONAL TEMPERATURE CHANGES. ALL OF THIS WAS IGNORED BY MANN.

The explanation for the growth spurt was that the bristlecone pine grows at the limit of moisture and fertility at altitude and hence shows strong responses to CO_2 fertilization. This was the point of the bristlecone study. THIS POINT COULD NOT HAVE BEEN MISSED BY MANN, BECAUSE IT IS THE TITLE OF THE PAPER FROM WHICH MANN DERIVED THE CRITICAL DATA TO SHOW THE POST-1910 TEMPERATURE RISE!

Mann et al. issued a "correction" later which admitted that their proxy data contained SOME ERRORS but "none of these errors affect our previously published results." This means that MANN WAS QUITE HAPPY TO PUBLISH WORK THAT HE HAD EITHER NOT CHECKED OR HE KNEW WAS WRONG. Mann was unable and unprepared to argue against the statistics of McIntyre and McKitrick and dogmatically stated that he was correct. He did not address the issue that bristlecone pine growth, his principal data set for his "hockey stick," was unrelated to temperature.

HOW BAD SCIENCE GETS PUBLISHED

Michael Mann's infamous Hockey Stick article was peer-reviewed and published in one of the world's most prestigious scientific journals. It also passed the allegedly much more detailed review when it attained prominence in the IPCC's Third Assessment Report. How was it that so many leading climatologists failed to notice its many flaws? What were these panels of experts thinking of?

To understand what happened, here is a brief explanation of what "peer review" entails. Peer review is basically a process whereby scientific or academic research is evaluated by qualified individuals within a related field prior to publication. Ostensibly, peer review methods are employed to improve accuracy and provide credibility. This is of particular concern when important national policies dealing with global warming are based on peer-reviewed research. The assumption is that peer-reviewed research has been tested to the degree that the results have been verified and validated. However, this assumption is not always the case.

Nobody really knows how many reviewers actually perform their duties with care. But attempts have been made to evaluate the efficacy of peer review as a way of identifying scientific error, and their conclusions have been largely unfavorable. Richards Smith, a former editor of the *British Medical Journal (BMJ)* has been a prominent critic of peer review:

> *We have little evidence on the effectiveness of peer review, but we have considerable evidence of its defects. In addition to being poor at detecting gross defects and almost useless for detecting fraud....*

Smith's successor at *BMJ*, Fiona Godlee, went a step further and with some of her colleagues, performed a trial in which eight errors were inserted into a genuine manuscript. This manuscript was then sent out to 420 reviewers. Of the 221 who responded, none found more than five of the mistakes, with the typical reviewer noting only two mistakes. One sixth of the respondents missed all eight errors.

The reasons for these failures become clear when we consider the nature of a peer review. **A PEER REVIEW NORMALLY CONSISTS OF ONLY READING A SCIENTIFIC OR ACADEMIC MANUSCRIPT THROUGH. IT DOES NOT INVOLVE OBTAINING THE DATA, REVIEWING THE CODE OR REPERFORMING CALCULATIONS.** Peer review is not due diligence in a way a business auditor would understand that term, and there is not pretence by journals that it is. It works as if an auditor read the company's annual report, but did not actually examine any of the underlying transactions or estimates.

Yet despite this, politicians and the public seem to somehow believe that if a paper passes peer review, it means it is correct. There seems to be a massive disconnect between the scientific community, and the politicians who rely on their findings to inform important policy decisions. Ross McKitrick, Professor of Economics at Canada's University of Guelph, revealed that, **"SOME GOVERNMENT STAFF ARE SURPRISED TO FIND OUT THAT PEER REVIEW DOES NOT INVOLVE CHECKING DATA AND CALCULATIONS, WHILE SOME ACADEMICS ARE SURPRISED THAT ANYONE THOUGHT IT DID."**

Only a few disciplines are now transforming the peer review process into a viable practice. For instance, the field of econometrics, which has long suffered from politicization and fraud, several journals have adopted clear and rigorous policies on archiving of data. At publications such as the *American Economic Review, Econometrica* and the *Journal of Money, Credit and Banking*, a manuscript that is submitted for publication will not be accepted **UNLESS DATA AND FULLY FUNCTIONAL CODE ARE AVAILABLE.** The failure of climatology journals to enact similar strict policies represents a serious flaw in the system of assurance that taxpayer-funded science is rigorous enough to base energy policy, especially when trillions of taxpayer dollars are at stake.

The "hockey stick" graphic used by the IPCC sent a very misleading message to the public. Furthermore, the 1996 IPCC report showed the Medieval Warming and the Little Ice Age. MANN'S "HOCKEY STICK" WAS USED IN THE IPCC'S 2001 REPORT AND THE MEDIEVAL WARMING AND LITTLE ICE AGE WERE EXPUNGED FROM THE RECORD OF MODERN CLIMATES. In the next IPCC report, the Medieval Warming and Little Ice Age mysteriously reappeared. The "HOCKEY STICK" DISAPPEARED AND REAPPEARED WITHOUT EXPLANATION BY THE IPCC!

This suggests that the IPCC knew that the "hockey stick" was invalid. This is a withering condemnation of the IPCC. The "hockey stick" was used as a backdrop for announcements about human-induced climate change. It is still used by Al Gore, and it is still used in talks by others, on websites and in publications by those claiming that the world is getting warmer due to human emissions. WERE ANY OF THOSE PEOPLE WHO VIEW THIS GRAPHIC TOLD THAT THE DATA BEFORE 1421 AD WAS BASED ON JUST ONE LONELY ALPINE TREE?

FEDERAL INVESTIGATION OF THE "HOCKEY STICK"

Mann had not released all his data and calculation methods to McIntyre and McKitrick, and was reported in public as stating that he would not be intimidated into disclosing the algorithm by which he obtained his results. THIS ATTRACTED THE INTEREST OF THE U.S. HOUSE ENERGY AND COMMERCE COMMITTEE. Its members read the McIntyre and McKitrick articles and became concerned about allegations that Mann had withheld adverse statistical results, and that his results depended upon bristlecone pine ring widths, well known to be a questionable measure of temperature. In June 2005, they sent questions to Mann and his co-authors about verification statistics and bristlecone pines, asked Mann for the algorithm he used, and asked pro forma questions about federal funds used in their research. This caused a storm with allegations of intimidation. Various learned societies, none of which had been offended by Mann's public refusal to provide full disclosure, were outraged that a House committee (representing the taxpayers who had paid for the results) should be trying to find out how Mann derived his results.

A turf war broke out. The House Science Committee felt its jurisdiction had been impinged upon. After a few months of battles, the House Science Committee asked the National Academy of Sciences (NAS) to evaluate criticism of Mann's work and to assess the larger issue of historical climate data reconstructions. The NAS agreed, but only under terms that precluded a direct investigation of the issues that prompted the original dispute – whether Mann et al. had withheld adverse results and whether the data and methodological information necessary for replication were available.

RQ Insight

"Consensus science" is an oxymoron. Science is the **LAST** place where you want a focus on consensus.

A **REAL** scientist always seeks new and different hypotheses to test their conclusions.

In the March 2006 hearings of the NAS, no claim of McIntyre and McKitrick was refuted. The NAS issued a press release in June 2006 stating:

> There is sufficient evidence from tree rings, boreholes, retreating glaciers and other 'proxies' of past surface temperature, to say with a high level of confidence, that the last few decades of the 20th Century were warmer than any comparable period in the last 400 years.

Basically, the NAS took THE POLITICALLY CORRECT ROUTE. Rather than publically declare Mann's data erroneous and vindicate McIntyre and McKitrick, the NAS failed to take a strong position either way, regardless of the truth of their findings. THIS PROVES ONCE AGAIN THAT MAN-MADE GLOBAL WARMING IS SUCH A POLITICALLY AND SOCIALLY CHARGED ISSUE THAT EVEN INSTITUTIONS LIKE THE NAS OPTS TO TOW THE LINE RATHER THAN TELL THE UNVARNISHED TRUTH.

But, luckily there are those who still believe in pursuing the truth even at the expense of popular opinion. In April of 2010, Virginia Attorney General Ken Cuccinelli took a stand and prepared to take on Michael Mann in legal battle. Mann was at the University of Virginia from 1999 to 2005, and during that time, he received nearly a half a million dollars in state grants for climate research. After so much controversy surrounding Mann's work, Attorney General Cuccinelli is investigating any possibility of data manipulation.

Since Mann conducted his research using state monies, Cuccinelli has the right to demand documents related to the research under the Fraud Against Taxpayers Act, a 2002 law designed to keep government workers honest. Cuccinelli has demanded that the University

EXPERTS AT "WINGING IT"

When the House Science Committee asked the National Academy of Sciences (NAS) to evaluate Mann's work, how exactly did the NAS do so, especially without access to Mann's data? In a speech after the findings were released, Dr. Gerald R. North, distinguished Professor of Atmospheric Sciences and Oceanography at Texas A&M University and member of the 12 member NAS panel, explained how the panel worked.

"We didn't do any research in this project, we just took a look at the papers that were existing and we tried to draw some kind of conclusions from them. So here we had twelve people around the table, all with very different backgrounds from one another and we just kind of winged it... that's what you do in that kind of expert panel."

– Dr. Gerald R. North

North said these words, not with any sense of dissatisfaction or of concern. His tone was matter-of-fact. It was just one more troubling revelation from the Hockey Stick affair. Faced with one of the most important scientific questions for decades, asked to study and report on a subject of incalculable economic, political and social importance, a group of distinguished scientists were asked by Congress to get around a table. What did they do? They talked about some papers and just "winged" it.

of Virginia provide a broad scope of documents related to Mann's work including any and all emails or written correspondence between or relating to Mann and more than 40 other climate scientists. In addition, the university has been asked to provide all documentation related to the five applications for the 484,875 dollars in grants and evidence of any documents that no longer exist along with proof of why, when and how they were destroyed or disappeared. Whether Cuccinelli finds his "smoking gun" against Mann remains to be seen. But, it is unlikely Virginia's Attorney General would embark on such a comprehensive investigation without a certain level of assurance that there was something to be found.

NEW PROOF IS IN THE EMAILS: A MASSIVE COVER-UP OF THE REAL DATA

In November of 2009, a number of emails became public between prominent American and British climate researchers that revealed just how insidious the man-made global warming cover-up had become. These emails showed discussions between researchers about whether certain scientific data should be released, as it didn't directly support the man-made global warming cause. In addition, there were sarcastic comments made in the emails about other scientists considered global warming "skeptics," who were referred to as "idiots."

One longtime climate researcher at the East Anglia Climate Research Unit said he had used what he called a "STATISTICAL TRICK" to hide the **DECLINE** in temperatures that his research had actually found. One of the most damning comments from the emails was one by Kevin Trenberth, a climatologist at the National Center for Atmospheric Research. He wrote, "THE FACT IS THAT WE CAN'T ACCOUNT FOR THE LACK OF WARMING AT THE MOMENT AND IT IS A TRAVESTY THAT WE CAN'T."

Even the director of the Climate Research Unit, Professor Phil Jones, was found to have commented in a note to an American colleague describing the death of a man-made global warming skeptic as "cheering news"; and a suggestion from Professor Jones that a "trick" is used to "HIDE THE DECLINE" in temperature. **ALL THE WHILE DURING HIS TENURE AT THE CLIMATE RESEARCH UNIT, HE RECEIVED 13 MILLION BRITISH POUNDS (OVER 21 MILLION DOLLARS) IN RESEARCH FUNDING!**

Professor Jones stood down as director of the Climate Research Unit pending an independent inquiry of the hacked email incident. During the investigation following the email

PREDICTION FALLACIES

Nobody believes a weather prediction twelve hours ahead. Now we're being asked to believe a prediction that goes out 100 years into the future? And make financial investments based on that prediction? Has everybody lost their minds?

Let's think back to people in 1900 in, say, New York. If they worried about people in 2000, what would they worry about? Probably: Where would people get enough horses? And what would they do about all the horseshit? Horse pollution was bad in 1900, think how much worse it would be a century later, with so many more people riding horses?

But of course, within a few years, nobody rode horses except for sport. And in 2000, France was getting 80 percent of its power from an energy source that was unknown in 1900. Germany, Switzerland, Belgium and Japan were getting more than 30% from this source, unknown in 1900. Remember, people in 1900 didn't know what an atom was. They didn't know its structure. They also didn't know what a radio was, or an airport, or a movie, or a television, or a computer, or a cell phone, or a jet, an antibiotic, a rocket, a satellite, an MRI, ICU, IUD, IBM, IRA, ERA, EEG, EPA, IRS, DOD, PCP, HTML, internet, interferon....

 Now. You tell me you can predict the world of 2100. Tell me it's even worth thinking about. Our models just carry the present into the future. They're bound to be wrong. Everybody who gives a moment's thought knows it.

Michael Crichton
Novelist and Harvard Medical School graduate

scandal, Professor Jones conceded the possibility that the world was warmer in medieval times than now, suggesting warming may not be a man-made phenomenon. Jones also admitted that for the past 15 years, there has been "NO STATISTICALLY SIGNIFICANT WARMING." He was forced to acknowledge that world was warmer back in medieval times than it is now, suggesting that global warming is not the man-made phenomenon he had strongly advocated.

More recently, the British House of Commons science and technology committee exonerated Dr. Jones, stating that the emphasis on Professor Jones had been largely misplaced and that he should be exonerated and allowed to resume his position as director of the Climate Research Unit. In a ridiculous statement by the committee's liberal democrat chairman, Phil Willis said: "THERE IS NO REASON WHY PROFESSOR JONES SHOULD NOT RESUME HIS POST. HE WAS CERTAINLY NOT CO-OPERATIVE WITH THOSE SEEKING TO GET DATA, BUT THAT WAS TRUE OF ALL THE CLIMATE SCIENTISTS."

Professor Jones aside, when these emails became public (earning the nickname "CLIMATEGATE"), it brought the truth to light that politicians, universities, individual scientists and the media have all conspired to keep any opposition to the man-made global warming cause under wraps. Patrick J. Michaels, a climatologist who has long faulted evidence pointing to human-driven warming, stated that the emails revealed an effort to suppress scientific information. He said, "THIS IS NOT A SMOKING GUN; THIS IS A MUSHROOM CLOUD."

RQ Insight

Despite the fact that so much of the "science" behind man-made global warming has been proven false, the legacy of the original bad science will continue. **THE INFAMOUS "HOCKEY STICK" CHART IS NOW IN MANY SCHOOL TEXTBOOKS** and is shared as fact to students from elementary school to graduate school. Even now that the hoax has been exposed, many people will **CONTINUE TO BELIEVE THE LIES THEY WERE ORIGINALLY TOLD.**

Even more damning are the conclusions put forth by A.W. Montford in his book, **The Hockey Stick Illusion: Climategate and the Corruption of Science**. At the conclusion of his book, Monford states:

> *...There are two clear conclusions to be drawn from the [Climategate] emails. Firstly, that senior climatologists have sought to undermine the peer review process and bully journals into suppressing dissenting views. This means that the scientific literature is no longer a representation of the state of human knowledge about the climate. It is a representation of what a small cabal of scientists feel is worthy of discussion. Secondly, the IPCC reports represent the outcome of a process in which a relatively small group of scientists produce a biased review of a literature they themselves have colluded to distort through gatekeeping and intimidation. The emails establish a pattern of behavior that is completely at odds with what the public has been told regarding the integrity of climate science and the rigour of the IPCC report-writing process. It is clear that the public can no longer trust what they have been told. What is less clear is what we, as ordinary citizens, can do in the face of the powerful, relentless forces of corrupted science, to set things right. Awareness, however, is the essential first step.*

MORE COVER-UPS

Beyond the email evidence, there is also another story of a Senior Operations Research Analyst for the Environmental Protection Agency who was targeted after submitting a report regarding changes to the Clean Air Act. The changes proposed would declare that carbon dioxide poses an "endangerment" to human health and the environment. Less than two weeks before, the agency formally submitted its pro-regulation recommendation to the White House. Cal Tech physics graduate and MIT Ph.D. economist, Dr. Alan Carlin, argued exactly as we have done earlier in this chapter. IN HIS 98-PAGE REPORT, HE STATED THAT THERE IS NO EVIDENCE THAT HUMAN-PRODUCED CARBON DIOXIDE DRIVES TEMPERATURES AND CLIMATE, RATHER THE SUN AND OCEANS DO. In his words, he warned the EPA not to make hasty "decisions based on a scientific hypothesis that does not appear to explain most of the available data." Dr. Carlin was informed by his supervisor that "the administrator and the administration have decided to move forward... and your comments do not help the legal or policy case for this decision." Further, Dr. Carlin was ordered not to have any direct communication with anyone outside of his small group at the EPA on the topic of climate change, and was informed that his report would not be shared with the agency group working on the topic. AFTER A 38-YEAR CAREER WITHIN THE EPA, DR. CARLIN IS NOW CONSIDERED A WHISTLE-BLOWER FOR REVEALING THE SUPPRESSION TACTICS THIS GOVERNMENT AGENCY HAS PUT ON ANY DATA THAT DOES NOT SUPPORT THE GOVERNMENT'S MAN-MADE GLOBAL WARMING AGENDA.

Another government agency has also earned a reputation for suppressing the man-made global warming doubts of its members. John Theon, retired NASA atmospheric scientist, has come out publically that he regretted the support he had earlier been obliged to give in favor of man-made global warming. Joining the rapidly growing ranks of international scientists abandoning the promotion of man-made global warming fears, Theon is the former supervisor of Dr. James Hanson (the chief climate scientist at NASA Goddard Institute for Space Studies (GISS)). Theon is the man who originally raised the alarm in 1988 in an appearance before Congress. He declared that Hansen "embarrassed NASA" with his alarming climate claims and said Hansen "was never muzzled." In an address to the International Conference on Climate Change in March 2009, Theon said:

> "I worked as the head of the NASA Weather and Climate Program, which included up to 300 scientists inside NASA, in academic and in the private sector… Jim Hansen had some very powerful political friends. Al Gore was a Senator… and subsequently became Vice President of the United States… Now there isn't too much a NASA person can do when he's up against that kind of challenge… In the early 1990's, I realized the whole thing was a great big fraud… recent developments have convinced me that it is my duty to speak out, and to help educate the public about what we're going to get into if we don't stop this nonsense."

BUT, REGARDLESS OF ALL OF THE DATA TO THE CONTRARY, MAN-MADE GLOBAL WARMING PROPONENTS ARE STILL TRYING TO SECURE AND PUSH THEIR AGENDA, OFTEN WITHOUT REGARD TO ETHICS OR MORALITY. For example, anyone who has done any kind of research on the internet has run across Wikipedia.com. Wikipedia is a free, web-based, collaborative, encyclopedia project whose 15 million articles have been written collaboratively by volunteers around the world. It is currently the largest and most popular general reference work on the internet. Wikipedia's articles can be edited by Wikipedia administrators.

One such administrator is William Connolley, a green party activist. HE HAS USED HIS ACCESS AS A WIKIPEDIA ADMINISTRATOR TO REWRITE WIKIPEDIA'S ENTRIES ON SEVERAL TOPICS INCLUDING GLOBAL WARMING, THE GREENHOUSE EFFECT, THE "HOCKEY STICK" WARMING CHART, CLIMATE MODELS AND GLOBAL COOLING. CONNOLLEY HAS EDITED THE WIKIPEDIA PIECE ON THE LITTLE ICE

AGE AND REWROTE HISTORY WITHOUT THE MEDIEVAL WARM PERIOD. The *Financial Post's*, Lawrence Solomon revealed the following about Connolley's Wikipedia activities.

> *"He rewrote articles on global warming and the scientists who were skeptical of the [man-made global warming].... If Connolley didn't like the subject of a certain article, he removed it – more than 500 articles of various descriptions disappeared at his hand. When he disapproved of the arguments that others were making, he often had them barred. Over 2,000 Wikipedia contributors who ran afoul of him found themselves blocked from making further contributions."*

Through his Wikipedia access, Connolley is attempting to control public access to information that is contrary to the man-made global warming agenda. Without any show of subtlety, Connolley has blatantly targeted some of the most distinguished climate scientists in his "editing efforts," including Richard Lindzen and Fred Singer. He has also gone after Willie Soon and Sallie Baliunas of the Harvard-Smithsonian Center for Astrophysics, authorities on the Medieval Warm Period.

Through his role as a Wikipedia administrator, Connolley is said to have created or rewritten 5,428 unique Wikipedia entries. To this day, Connolley continues to make edits to numerous Wikipedia articles in an overt attempt to keep the public blind to the scientific truth behind the man-made global warming hoax. As of early 2010, he has already "edited" Wikipedia articles including "Public opinion on climate change," "Climate," "Scientific opinion on climate change," "RealClimate," "Global cooling," "Climate change" and the biography of scientist William M. Gray (prominent hurricane forecaster and man-made global warming skeptic), writing that Gray's "views on global warming are controversial."

SPINNING THE TALE OF MAN-MADE GLOBAL WARMING

There are still plenty of scientists willing to support man-made global warming. Why? Because that's where the grant money is! SINCE 1989, OVER 79 BILLION DOLLARS OF THE TAXPAYERS' MONEY HAS BEEN SPENT ON FEDERAL POLICIES RELATED TO CLIMATE CHANGE, INCLUDING SCIENCE AND TECHNOLOGY RESEARCH, ADMINISTRATION, PROPAGANDA CAMPAIGNS, FOREIGN AID AND TAX BREAKS. So, naturally, in order to keep their research monies flowing, these scientists get really nervous when their findings are actually disproving man-made global warming. As early as 1989, scientists were admitting that, despite data to the contrary, they needed to keep their pushing dramatic and dire forecasts in order to keep the illusion of man-made global warming alive.

"To capture the public imagination we have to offer up some scary scenarios, make simplified dramatic statements and make little mention of any doubts one might have. Each of us has to strike the right balance between being effective and being honest."

Dr. Stephen Schneider, *Discover*, October 1989

Scientists, the government, and the media have all intentionally furthered the doomsday predictions of man-made global warming.

"Unless we announce disasters, no one will listen."

Sir John Houghton, [Former] Chairman
Intergovernmental Panel on Climate Change Scientific Working Group, 1994

With all of this pressure to keep a lid on any contrary data, it is not easy for scientists to go against the man-made global warming main-stream. Like Galileo in 1610 advancing the theory that it was the sun, not the earth, that was the center of universe, many scientists have been persecuted for their non-conforming studies. They might not be arrested and forced to recant like Galileo, but they are finding it difficult to find a voice for their findings, and are receiving significant censure from their peers and the media.

Yet, more and more scientists refuse to be cowed. IN 1998, THE GLOBAL WARMING PETITION PROJECT BEGAN TO BE CIRCULATED. Its purpose is to demonstrate that the claim of "settled science" and an overwhelming "consensus " in favor of the hypothesis of human-caused global warming and consequent climatological damage is INCORRECT. The petition opposes claims by publicists at the United Nations, Al Gore and their supporters that only a few "skeptics" remain – skeptics who are still unconvinced about the existence of a catastrophic man-made global warming emergency.

In August 2007, Physicist Frederick Seitz, President of the U.S. National Academy of Sciences and of Rockefeller University, wrote a letter in support of the petition. A VIGOROUS SUPPORTER OF THE PETITION PROJECT, PROFESSOR SEITZ RECEIVED THE NATIONAL MEDAL OF SCIENCE, THE COMPTON AWARD, THE FRANKLIN MEDAL, AND NUMEROUS OTHER AWARDS, INCLUDING HONORARY DOCTORATES FROM 32 UNIVERSITIES AROUND THE WORLD. Dr. Seitz REVIEWED and APPROVED the article by Robinson, Robinson, and Soon that we have heavily referenced in this book. The petition states:

We urge the United States government to reject the global warming agreement that was written in Kyoto, Japan in December, 1997, and any other similar proposals. The proposed limits on greenhouse gases would harm the environment, hinder the advance of science and technology, and damage the health and welfare of mankind.

There is no convincing scientific evidence that human release of carbon dioxide, methane, or other greenhouse gasses is causing or will, in the foreseeable future, cause catastrophic heating of the Earth's atmosphere and disruption of the Earth's climate. Moreover, there is substantial scientific evidence that increases in atmospheric carbon dioxide produce many beneficial effects upon the natural plant and animal environments of the Earth.

As of January 2010, the petition above has been signed by **17,100 AMERICAN SCIENTISTS, TWO-THIRDS OF WHICH HOLD ADVANCED DEGREES.** The signers of the petition represent more than a few skeptics, as claimed by Al Gore and others. They are, in fact, thousands of like-minded scientists – including physicists, geophysicists, climatologists, meteorologists, oceanographers and environmental scientists – who are convinced that man-made global warming is without scientific validity and that government action on the basis of this hypothesis would have absolutely no impact on global warming and would cost American taxpayers trillions of tax dollars.

But despite the petition and the ever increasing scientific data to the contrary, our government will not be swayed from its course. It continues to pursue the regulation and limitation of carbon emissions under the guise of saving the planet.

OBAMA, NASA AND THE CONTINUING CLIMATE CRAZE

In February of 2010, President Obama announced his 2011 budget would eliminate among other things, NASA's Constellation program, the program that would return astronauts to the moon. Instead, he added ROUGHLY **6** BILLION DOLLARS TO **NASA'S** BUDGET TO PURSUE A NEW, MUCH MORE TERRESTRIAL MISSION: MONITORING EARTH CLIMATE CHANGES IN AN EFFORT TO DOCUMENT GLOBAL WARMING!

Ordering the shuttle program to end, Obama has now crippled the future of spaceflight in order to further gather evidence of the non-existent threat of man-made global warming. "There will be no lunar landers, no moon bases, no Constellation program at all," Robert Black and Mark Mathews of the Orlando Sentinel wrote. "In the meantime, the White House will direct NASA to concentrate on Earth-science projects – principally, research and MONITORING CLIMATE CHANGE." Obama's decision was made despite conclusive proof that science behind global warming is suspect, including the "Climategate" release of more than 1,000 emails documenting that prominent scientists working for the United Nation's Intergovernmental Panel on Climate Control were falsifying documents in their efforts to fuel the flames of climate change hysteria.

Oh, by the way, now that the shuttle program is no more, NASA was forced to sign a 335 million dollar contract to buy six extra seats on the Russian Soyuz spacecraft to launch American and partner astronauts into space once the space shuttle fleet is retired. The new deal allows NASA to pay the Russians Federal Space Agency for six round-trip rides to and from the Internatinal Space Station in 2013 and 2014. That averages to about 55.8 million dollars per trip!

Even more troubling in times where terrorists actively target our nation and its citizens like the Fort Hood shooting, the airline underwear bomber of December 2009 and the Times Square bombing attempt in early May 2010, PRESIDENT OBAMA HAS TASKED THE CENTRAL INTELLIGENCE AGENCY TO INVESTIGATE GLOBAL WARMING. THE CIA'S ENVIRONMENTAL SURVEILLANCE, MEASUREMENTS OF EARTH DATA FOR ENVIRONMENTAL ANALYSIS (MEDEA), WHICH OPERATES OUT OF THE CIA'S NATIONAL RECONNAISSANCE OFFICE, HAS NOW BEEN TASKED BY THE OBAMA ADMINISTRATION TO SUPPLY CLASSIFIED SATELLITE INTELLIGENCE TO A GROUP OF GOVERNMENT-CHOSEN SCIENTISTS TO MEASURE CLIMATE CHANGES, INCLUDING ARCTIC SEA ICE. This ridiculous waste of intelligence resources will hopefully only lead to a waste of tax dollars and prove to be a fatal error as the CIA is so busy monitoring the weather that potential future security threats go unthwarted.

UN Copenhagen Climate Conference 2009

In November of 2009, the UN Climate Change Conference was held in Copenhagen, Denmark. This massive conference, which attracted more than 15,000 delegates, 45,000 activists, 5,000 journalists and 98 world leaders, was basically a two-week environmental catastrophe. The stated goals for the conference were to:

1. Make clear how much developed countries, such as the U.S., Australia, and Japan, will limit their greenhouse gas emissions.
2. Determine how, and to what degree, developing countries can limit their emissions without limiting economic growth.
3. Explore options for "stable and predictable financing" from developed countries that can help them reduce greenhouse gas emissions and adapt to climate change.
4. Identify ways to ensure developing countries are treated as equal partners in decision-making, particularly when it comes to technology and finance.

None of these goals were achieved. Several leaders from developing countries walked out of the conference in a huff. President Obama and Danish Prime Minister Lars Lokke Rasmussen both conceded that the conference did not produce any legally binding treaty. For this, Dr. Jim Hansen, NASA scientist and climate change activist since the 1980s, is grateful. Before the conference, Dr. Hansen attested that any deal emerging from the conference would be so flawed it would be better to just have the talks collapse. But the conference did result in some profound consequences. Again, these were not intended results, but they are very significant.

- The conference cost over **200 MILLION DOLLARS**, including **10 MILLION DOLLARS** in airfare, over **31 MILLION DOLLARS** in hotels, and **5.25 MILLION DOLLARS** in food. The majority of this money came from, you guessed it, **TAXPAYERS**. Supporters of the conference say this money is only a drop in the ocean compared to the "benefits of preventing dangerous climate change!"

- Majken Friss Jorgensen, managing director of Copenhagen's biggest limousine company, stated in an article in the U.K.'s Telegraph, "We thought they were not going to need many cars, due to it being a climate convention. But, it seems that somebody last week looked at the weather report." It was a bit of a cold, rainy week so well over 1,200 limousines were made use of during the conference, more than are in all of Denmark. More limousines had to be driven in hundreds of miles from Germany and Sweden to accommodate delegate requests. **ONLY FIVE OF ALL OF THESE VEHICLES MADE USE OF ELECTRIC OR HYBRID TECHNOLOGY!**

- While belaboring the public about how they should lower their living standards, pay higher taxes on all forms of travel, and make personal sacrifices in order to save the planet from the "threat" of CO_2, **CONFERENCE ATTENDEES TOOK 140 PRIVATE JETS TO THE CONFERENCE.** The planes were forced to drop off their passengers and then fly right back out of Copenhagen either back home or to other countries because Copenhagen's airport had simply run out of places to park.

- Finally, as only the Danish can, the Mayor of Copenhagen tried to enforce his own emissions limits by sending a letter to hotels across the city, urging delegates and guests at the conference to "be sustainable, don't buy sex." **PROSTITUTES RESPONDED BY OFFERING FREE SEX TO ANY CONFERENCE ATTENDEE WHO PRODUCED A COPY OF THE MAYOR'S LETTER.** This practice gave new meaning to the term **"CARBON DATING."**

In all, the UN Copenhagen Climate Conference generated a **41,000 TON CARBON FOOTPRINT, EQUAL TO THE ANNUAL FOOTPRINT OF 40 OF THE WORLD'S SMALLEST COUNTRIES COMBINED.** That's correct! Those attending the two-week 2009 Copenhagen Climate Conference had a bigger carbon footprint than the 40 smallest countries in the world **FOR AN ENTIRE YEAR.**

MAN-MADE GLOBAL WARMING
HOAX

part three **| THE CONSEQUENCES OF THE MAN-MADE GLOBAL WARMING HOAX**

Part two of this book was dedicated to describing in detail how and why man-made global warming is a hoax; a deliberate manipulation of scientific data combined with biased media coverage to gather public support for a political agenda. The third part of this book will show in detail how the U.S. government has leveraged public support of man-made global warming to institute various policies that will not only threaten American livelihoods, but their very lives.

In part three, we will first look at how the government continues to pursue corn-based ethanol as an alternative to carbon-based fuel despite the fact that corn-based ethanol production is far more pernicious environmentally and economically than gasoline. Then, we will address the unbelievable costs associated with our government's pursuit of the carbon-emissions cap and trade program that will costs American's families thousands of extra dollars each year while the government cashes in and many man-made global warming propagandists cash in. Finally, we will address the hidden lethality in the government's continued pursuit of CAFE fuel economy standards and how, as a result of lighter-weight cars, thousands of American's have already lost their lives on the roads.

CHAPTER EIGHT |

EHTHANOL & THE MAN-MADE GLOBAL WARMING HOAX

Taking advantage of the public support it has generated through the man-made global warming hoax, the government has been able to pursue various policies targeted at different products and industries. One such product is CORN-BASED ETHANOL as an alternative and/or supplement to gasoline. The assumption is that the use of ethanol would result in less CO_2 released into the environment by man, and also result in using less oil for gasoline.

Ethanol (ethyl alcohol) is the main ingredient in alcoholic beverages. Residues found on pottery discovered in Northern China suggest that we have been getting drunk on ethanol for over 9000 years. But, it is not ethanol for alcohol that the government is supporting at the moment. IT IS ETHANOL AS FUEL. IT PRODUCES LESS CO_2 AND ENABLES US TO USE LESS OIL – IN THEORY.

In the United States, ethanol has been used for fuel for more than 100 years. Henry Ford's famous Model T was designed to run on either gasoline or pure ethanol. Ethanol cars were

driven into the 1920's and 1930's until gasoline became the preferred fuel source. Ethanol's use as fuel waxed and waned over the years until it found new life as a result of the energy crisis in the late 1970's. THE ENERGY TAX ACT OF 1978 PROVIDED ECONOMIC INCENTIVES AND SUBSIDIES FOR THE DEVELOPMENT OF ETHANOL. The banning of leaded gasoline in 1986 further expanded the interest in ethanol as a non-petroleum-based fuel source.

Then, in 2007, when Congress passed the Energy Independence and Security Act (EISA), they mandated that we make use of 35

U.S. Fuel Ethanol Production

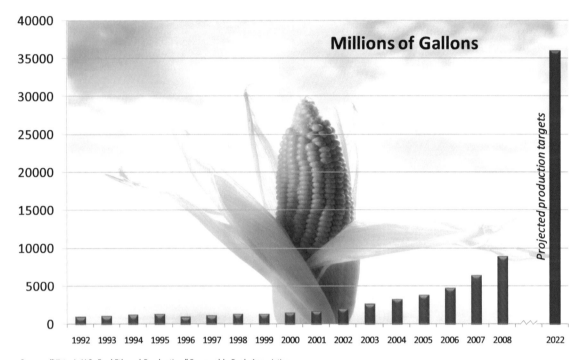

Source: "Historic U.S. Fuel Ethanol Production," Renewable Fuels Association.
Available at http://www.ethanolrfa/industry/statistics/
Target production for 2002 (36 billion gallons) according to H.R.6 (passed by the Senate June 21, 2007)

billion gallons of alternative fuels by 2017. The EISA provided significant tax incentives and grants to ethanol producers in order to help reach this goal. THE NEW 35 BILLION GALLONS STANDARD EQUATED TO A FIVE-FOLD INCREASE FROM THE PRODUCTION GOALS AT THE TIME. Why would our government want to push such a dramatic increase in alternative fuel production, especially ethanol? They publically stated their intentions as follows:

INTENTION ONE: **GREENER FUEL**

> We were told that ethanol would be instrumental against the growing problem of man-made global warming. We were told that ethanol would help lead the way in developing "greener" energy alternatives, help reduce our consumption of non-renewable resources, and protect our environment.

INTENTION TWO: **NO MORE DEPENDENCE ON FOREIGN OIL**

> The government told us that ethanol would play a key role in reducing our nation's dependence on foreign, especially Middle Eastern, oil. Ethanol would help us regain our self-sufficiency when it came to our energy requirements, and producing/consuming

ethanol as fuel would be critical to not only our economic stability, but was a matter of national security.

INTENTION THREE: SUPPORT FOR DOMESTIC AGRICULTURE

Not only would ethanol reduce our need for foreign oil and provide cleaner and more efficient fuel, its production would help breathe new life into our ailing farm industry. We would revitalize our nation's farmers by using their hard-won harvests, and producing the next generation of environmentally-friendly fuels.

Viewed in this way, how could the increased production of ethanol be anything but a win-win scenario? The government seems to be promoting a positive, long-term investment into our nation's future. But, DOES ETHANOL DELIVER WHAT THE GOVERNMENT CONTINUES TO SUGGEST IT WILL? I think you will be surprised. First, let us take a quick look at ethanol production in our country.

U.S. ETHANOL SOURCE OF CHOICE: CORN

While there are other sources of ethanol (sugar cane, switch grass, palm, etc.), U.S. ethanol is predominantly made from corn. Why corn? THE UNITED STATES IS ALREADY THE LARGEST

U.S. Corn Use
Marketing Year 2008/09

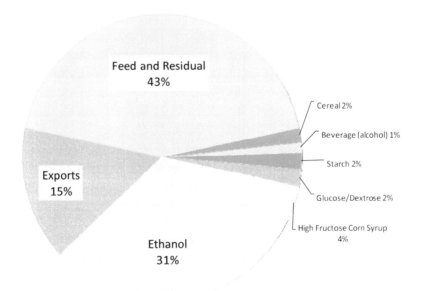

Source: "Feed Outlook." Economic Research service, USDA, October 14, 2009, Baker, Allen and Lutman.
Available at http://usda.mannlib.cornell.edu/usda/current/FDS/FDS-10-14-2009.pdf

CORN-PRODUCING NATION IN THE WORLD, CONTRIBUTING ALMOST **40%** TO GLOBAL CORN PRODUCTION. So, when choosing a source for ethanol, corn was considered the top choice largely because of the political and lobbying considerations, as will be demonstrated later.

For many of us, ethanol is already a part of daily life. ABOUT **3.5** PERCENT OF THE **U.S.** FUEL SUPPLY IS ETHANOL. This may not seem like much, but when you consider that, in 2006, Americans burned upwards of five billion gallons of this corn-based fuel and that this was twice our consumption from four years earlier, you may begin to appreciate how quickly ethanol is taking hold in our country.

The majority of the ethanol we currently use is a 90/10 percent gas to ethanol mix, called E10. Higher ethanol blends do exist such as E85 (a 15/85 percent gas to ethanol) and these higher ethanol blends are slowly gaining traction here in the U.S. But, for now, E10 remains our primary ethanol product.

As of January 2010, there are 189 operational ethanol refineries in the U.S., with 11 more under construction. The combined production capacity of these refineries is 12 billion gallons of ethanol a year. AT THE MOMENT, THIS IS **23** BILLION GALLONS **LESS** THAN THE **35** BILLION GALLON TARGET SET BY THE ENERGY INDEPENDENCE AND SECURITY ACT (EISA) IN **2007.**

State governments are throwing their weight behind ethanol, as well.

- Ten states are now requiring the use of ethanol-blended fuel.
- Twelve states have some form of retail pump incentive for ethanol.
- Twenty-two states offer some type of incentive for ethanol producers.

The U.S. is already the top ethanol distiller in the world, surpassing Brazil, who produces its ethanol from sugarcane. New government standards are slated to increase our pace of ethanol production.

But beyond simply mandating increased production and use standards for ethanol, our government is also providing extensive financial support for this corn-based fuel. Of all federal subsidies set aside for renewable energy sources in 2007, 76 percent of the tax benefits and 66 percent of all federal subsidies were allotted to ethanol!

The cost of ethanol for tax payers continues to grow with each gallon sold. Currently, there is a **0.51** CENT SUBSIDY PER GALLON which equates to $5 billion a year in 2010. THIS ANNUAL **5** BILLION DOLLAR SUBSIDY IS MORE THAN WHAT IS SPENT ON ALL ENVIRONMENTAL PROTECTION PROGRAMS FOR SOIL, WATER AND WILDLIFE HABITAT BY THE **U.S.** DEPARTMENT OF AGRICULTURE. Additional subsidies and increases in the amount of ethanol-blended fuels required to be consumed by American drivers is high on the agenda for the corn ethanol lobby. It is a well

Federal Energy Tax Credits
for Ethanol 2007

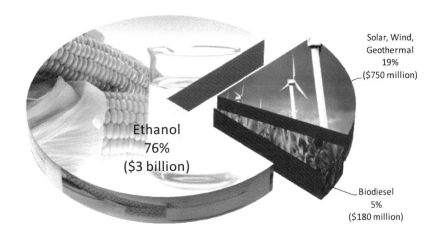

Ethanol
76%
($3 billion)

Solar, Wind,
Geothermal
19%
($750 million)

Biodiesel
5%
($180 million)

Source: "Ethanol's Federal Subsidy Grab Leaves Little for Solar, Wind and Geothermal Energy, Environmental Working Group. January 8, 2009.
Available at http://www.ewg.org/reports/Ethanols-Federal-Subsidy-Grab-Leaves-Little_for_SolarWind-And-Geothermal-Energy+

accepted reality that the government intends to intensify its already staggering support of corn-based ethanol.

THE UNINTENDED CONSEQUENCES OF CORN-BASED ETHANOL

So, what's the problem? Ethanol is simply **NOT** living up to the promises initially made by our government. In addition, several unintended consequences to the production and consumption of corn-based ethanol have been uncovered – most of which the government is refusing to address!

DEPENDENCE ON FOREIGN OIL REMAINS

Ethanol will simply never be able to offset our need for foreign oil. For an explanation why, let's consider U.S. corn production as a whole. CURRENTLY, A LITTLE OVER **30** PERCENT OF OUR TOTAL CORN PRODUCTION IS USED TO PRODUCE ETHANOL. The remaining 70 percent is used mostly for feed, residual, exports and food products.

A Congressional Research Service study calculated how much foreign oil could be displaced if our **ENTIRE** corn crop was dedicated to the production of ethanol. Their findings showed that the ethanol produced would equate to LESS THAN **15** PERCENT of our national gasoline consumption.

RQ Insight

A University of Minnesota study found that even if all of our corn **AND SOYBEAN** fields were utilized for ethanol production (as unlikely as that would be), the reduction in gasoline use would be only 18 percent.

When they considered how much energy would be needed to produce the ethanol, the gasoline demand would **ONLY BE REDUCED BY 5 PERCENT!**

What would it take for ethanol to actually displace 30% of our gasoline demand? It would take over 140 million acres of corn to produce the appropriate amount of ethanol. THE PROBLEM IS THAT IN 2009, OUR TOTAL CORN HARVEST WAS ONLY 80 MILLION ACRES. THAT LEAVES 60 MILLION ACRES OF LAND THAT WOULD HAVE TO BE REDEDICATED TO CORN FIELDS JUST TO PRODUCE ENOUGH ETHANOL TO OFFSET ONLY 30% OF OUR GASOLINE CONSUMPTION. This is not counting the acreage needed to produce our other corn-based products like animal feed and food! As summarized in the 2007 Congressional Research Service Report, "barring a drastic realignment of U.S. field crop production patterns, corn-based ethanol's potential as a petroleum import substitute appears to be limited by a crop area constraint."

We currently do not have the land to make enough ethanol to offset foreign oil. Could we find it? Perhaps, and given the government's push for ethanol, we have already started rededicating land for more corn to produce ethanol. But, where will this other land come from? Will we take land away from other crops? Will we use forest land? We would probably need to do both, and the repercussions of doing either are potentially devastating and the result will be that WE STILL WON'T OFFSET OUR NEED FOR FOREIGN OIL.

Why? According to Cato Institute Senior Fellow, Jerry Taylor, "it may very well be that BIOFUELS DISPLACE MORE DOMESTIC OIL THAN FOREIGN OIL, because foreign oil is cheaper to produce than domestic crude…. biofuels will displace more expensive sources of crude oil, which come primarily from the U.S. and Canada, not the Persian Gulf." The bottom line is that our government is pursuing a biofuel alternative in corn-based ethanol that will never really affect our consumption of foreign oil. It is and will continue to be a hollow promise.

ETHANOL HAS GREATLY INCREASED THE POWER OF THE AGRICULTURE LOBBY

The government's push for ethanol is helping the farm industry, but probably not in the way most voters would imagine it does. If you picture family farmers patriotically working their lands and finally getting fair prices for their hard-won harvests, you would be correct if you substituted the family farmer with large to mid-sized agribusiness conglomerates.

Large industrial farms are receiving the lion's share of government monies to the tune of 628,000 dollars a year going to the top one percent of all corn growers. THE SMALLER, FAMILY OWNED FARMS ARE RECEIVING ONLY A SMALL PIECE OF THE SUBSIDY PIE, WITH JUST 13 PERCENT OF UNITED STATES DEPARTMENT OF AGRICULTURE CORN SUBSIDIES GOING TO THE BOTTOM 80 PERCENT OF CORN GROWERS.

When it comes to subsidies for the production and distribution of corn-based ethanol, things become more challenging. With all of the federal and state subsidies that cover almost every production input and production stage of ethanol, coming up with a solid number for

Concentration of Federal Payments
1995-2006

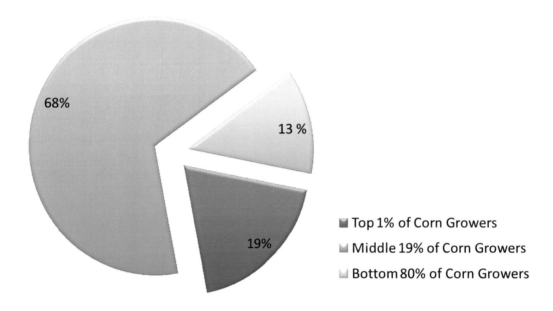

68%

13 %

19%

■ Top 1% of Corn Growers

◩ Middle 19% of Corn Growers

◩ Bottom 80% of Corn Growers

Source: Environmental working Group Farm Subsidy Data Base. Available at:
http://farm.ewg.org/farm/progdetail.php?fips=00000&progcode=corn&page=conc

how much ethanol costs taxpayers is difficult. However, the International Institute for Sustainable Development conducted a study in 2006 which took up this challenge. Researcher David Koplow estimated that government support for ethanol ranges between 6.3 billion dollars and 8.7 billion dollars per year. If we took the middle point between Koplow's estimates and factor in that just one agribusiness conglomerate, ARCHER DANIELS MIDLAND (ADM), CONTROLS ABOUT A THIRD OF THE ETHANOL MARKET, WE COULD ESTIMATE THAT ADM WOULD RECEIVE OVER TWO BILLION DOLLARS IN SUBSIDIES IN ONE YEAR.

All of this makes ADM and its competitors highly motivated to pursue further government support of ethanol. Since 1990, ADM has reported over eight million dollars in political campaign contributions. Shortly before President Bill Clinton tried to push standardizing a minimum of 10 percent of ethanol in all gasoline, ADM's former chairman, Dwayne Andreas was reported to have contributed 100,000 dollars at a presidential fund-raiser. Over the years, ADM had given money to Senator Bob Dole, President Clinton, President Bush, President Carter, Michel Dukakis, Jack Kemp and Jesse Jackson, among others.

ADM also leveraged its political influence via the AARC (Alternative Agriculture Research and Commercialization) Corp. AARC is a venture capital firm owned by the US Department of Agriculture. Their aim is to further the development of environmentally-friendly non-food products from farm and forest materials. IN 1995, THEN CHAIRMAN, MARTIN ANDREAS, STEERED 2.4 MILLION DOLLARS OF RESEARCH MONEY TO ADM PROJECTS AND BUSINESS INTERESTS. IF THE NAME SOUNDS FAMILIAR, MARTIN IS THE NEPHEW OF THEN ADM CHAIR, DWAYNE ANDREAS.

In the government's support for ethanol, they have provided the agriculture industry with a powerful opportunity to push legislation that is in their best interests – not necessarily the best interests of the country or our environmental concerns. It's no coincidence that presidential candidates feel pushed to promote ethanol. The first and arguably the most important presidential caucus of any election year does take place in Iowa – a corn-producing state. In 1976, presidential candidate Jimmy Carter promised high ethanol subsidies to Iowa corn growers, and every presidential campaign since, both Republican and Democrat candidates, make the same promises.

ETHANOL IS NOT GREEN

ETHANOL IS NOT, IN ACTUALITY, A GREENER FUEL THAN GASOLINE. In this section, we will examine ethanol from four "green-relevant" angles: energy production, emissions, fuel efficiency and environmental impact.

ENERGY PRODUCTION

First, consider THAT A GALLON OF PURE ETHANOL HAS 33 PERCENT LESS ENERGY THAN A GALLON OF GASOLINE! Translated, if you were to put pure ethanol into your car (not recommended), you would only go 67 percent as far on that tank of ethanol as you would go on a tank full of gasoline.

Furthermore, ethanol has been found to be a negative energy fuel. It takes more energy to produce ethanol (131,000 BTUs) than ethanol can generate (77,000 BTUs). In addition, unlike oil, ethanol cannot be transported by pipeline because the ethanol collects too many impurities in the process. So, it must be transported by truck, which adds to the energy expenditure required for its production and distribution.

RQ Insight

Motorists also pay a great deal of money on repair costs related to ethanol-blend fuel damage. Lexus, Toyota, BMW and others have spent millions on recalls and warranty-related repairs due to ethanol-blends. Boat owners have been hard hit as ethanol eats its way through the resins in fiberglass tanks. And, if you own landscaping tools beware, using more than **10% ETHANOL IN THESE SMALL ENGINE DEVICES VOIDS THEIR FACTORY WARRANTIES.**

L THINK.

The emissions history of ethanol refineries is nothing about "green." Just like any other refinery, ethanol refineries contribute significantly to air pollution. The Environmental Protection Agency (EPA) considers ethanol plants to be major sources of air pollution if they emit more than 100 tons of toxic chemicals a year. WHAT MIGHT COME AS A SURPRISE GIVEN THAT THESE REFINERIES PRODUCE AN "ENVIRONMENTALLY-FRIENDLY" BIOFUEL IS THAT SEVERAL OF THESE FACILITIES HAVE BEEN PENALIZED FOR **NOT** MEETING THE **100** TON BASIC GOVERNMENT EMISSIONS STANDARD.

In 2002, twelve ethanol refineries were fined by federal and state officials for violations of the Clean Air Act. In 2003, Archer Daniels Midland (ADM), the largest ethanol producer in the United States, reached a landmark settlement with the EPA. ADM was accused of failing to accurately estimate its emissions from hundreds of processing units. ADM also expanded other units without the installation of required air pollution controls. It is estimated that in order to fully comply with the settlement in all of their 52 plants located in 16 states, it would cost ADM 340 million dollars.

In 2005, Cargill, Inc., the second largest ethanol producer in the U.S., reached an agreement with the EPA to implement system-wide environmental improvements at its 27 nation-wide plants. Cargill also had to pay 1.6 million dollars to both federal and state governments for its violations against EPA standards. The total cost for Cargill to meet all of the standards put in place by the injunction was estimated to be 130 million dollars over 10 years. Under the settlement, Cargill was to reduce its air pollution by at least 24,950 tons a year.

HOWEVER, IN A BIZARRE TURN OF EVENTS, IN **2006** THE EPA CHOSE TO **EASE** EMISSIONS RESTRICTIONS FOR ETHANOL REFINERIES TO THE TUNE OF **150** PERCENT. The only reasonable explanation for this shift in policy is to allow refineries to switch to coal for their ethanol production. Many refineries had been using natural gas, which is more expensive than coal. Coal would make ethanol cheaper but far dirtier. But, the EPA has signed off in any case. ETHANOL REFINERIES CAN NOW PRODUCE MORE TOXIC EMISSIONS WITHOUT GOVERNMENT CENSURE AND, AS MORE REFINERIES COME ON LINE, ANY HOPE FOR A "GREENER" FUEL IS RAPIDLY DISAPPEARING.

Once ethanol gets into the tanks of our cars, the "green" situation does not improve. According to the EPA and the National Research Council, adding ethanol to gasoline is not effective for reducing emissions of green house gases. IN SOME CASES, ETHANOL-BLEND FUELS GENERATED HIGHER EMISSIONS (AN AVERAGE OF **7.7** PERCENT) THAN GASOLINE. Ethanol has been found to generate higher levels of other toxic emissions like formaldehyde, benzene and cancer-causing aldehydes (which are found in cigarette smoke). These ethanol emissions have been linked to respiratory issues, blood disorders, and pregnancy problems. ONE STUDY HAS SUGGESTED THAT SWITCHING TO HIGH ETHANOL-FUEL BLENDS LIKE E85 COULD RESULT IN HIGHER OZONE RELATED MORTALITY, HOSPITALIZATION AND ASTHMA RATES (9 PERCENT HIGHER IN LOS ANGELES AND 4 PERCENT HIGHER ACROSS THE U.S.).

FUEL EFFICIENCY

Ethanol actually reduces fuel efficiency in cars. THE FUEL BLEND OF E10 IS ABOUT 4 PERCENT LESS EFFICIENT THAN GASOLINE. HIGHER FUEL BLENDS LIKE E85 HAVE BEEN FOUND TO BE OVER 25 PERCENT LESS FUEL EFFICIENT THAN UNLEADED GASOLINE. The government is forcing us to spend more money at the pump and drive fewer miles with it.

ENVIRONMENTAL IMPACT

Corn is the least sustainable of all common raw biofuel materials. Yet, the U.S. continues to pursue an aggressive increase in the production of corn-based ethanol. Corn is a nutrient-intensive crop characterized by extensive soil tillage and the heavy application of fertilizers and pesticides. OVER 40 PERCENT OF ALL COMMERCIAL FERTILIZERS ARE USED IN THE PRODUCTION OF CORN. It has been estimated farmers that use twice the amount of nitrogen fertilizer than their crops can actually absorb. Growing corn causes significant strain on soil, causing degradation and erosion. The additional need for corn for ethanol production will only increase these issues.

The increased profit opportunities provided by government support of ethanol could also encourage corn growers to skip environmentally responsible crop rotation cycles. Rather, they are more inclined to simply plant corn year after year. Crop rotation is designed to allow soil to regenerate between crops, as one type of crop draws different nutrients from the soil than the next. As monocropping occurs, farmers rely on even heavier use of fertilizers and other chemicals to produce crops. This, in turn, leads to eutrophication of our nation's water systems.

Eutrophication is a process whereby an increased concentration of nutrients in water causes excessive plant growth (algae and other "nuisance" plants). This enhanced plant growth reduces dissolved oxygen in the water, making it impossible for most other aquatic life to survive. THE RUNOFF FROM THE CORN BELT STATES HAS ALREADY CONTRIBUTED SIGNIFICANTLY TO THE MISSISSIPPI DELTA/GULF OF MEXICO DEAD ZONE – AN ALMOST 8,000 SQUARE MILE AREA WHERE THE WATER OXYGEN LEVELS HAVE BEEN SO DEPLETED, LIFE CANNOT EXIST. THIS EQUATES TO AN AREA THE SIZE OF THE STATE OF NEW JERSEY. The contamination of water can also be seen closer to home. Nitrogen-based fertilizer is the most commonly used fertilizer in the farming

The Gulf of Mexico Dead Zone

Located at the mouth of the Mississippi River, the Gulf of Mexico dead zone is an area of hypoxic water (less than 2 ppm dissolved oxygen) that varies in size, but can cover over 8,000 square miles. Dead zones can be found across the world, but the Gulf of Mexico dead zone is one of the largest in the world. Others in the United States include an area off the coast of Oregon, the Chesapeake Bay and one in Lake Erie.

Dead zones occur when massive amounts of nutrients and phosphorus are dumped into water systems causing an overabundance in algae growth. These algae blooms absorb so much oxygen from the water surrounding them that other aquatic life cannot survive. This, in turn, disrupts the food chain within that ecosystem, having a domino effect on other marine life. Dead zones fluctuate seasonally as they are heavily influenced by farming practices. Weather conditions such as hurricanes and flooding also affect dead zone sizes.

The Gulf of Mexico dead zone was caused by our nation's farming industry. The major farming states in the Mississippi River Valley all contribute, including Minnesota, Iowa, Illinois, Wisconsin, Missouri, Tennessee, Arkansas, Mississippi and Louisiana.

The run-off of fertilizers, soil erosion, animal wastes and sewage carry nitrogen and phosphorus to the river and down into the Gulf of Mexico, resulting in massive fish kills. *The Gulf of Mexico is a major source area for the seafood industry. It supplies 72 percent of U.S. harvested shrimp, 66 percent of harvested oysters and 16 percent of commercial fish.* In 1995, the government provided disaster relief for the fishing industry in that area to the tune of 15 million dollars. The potential impact of a continued growth in corn production for ethanol on the Dead Zone and other ecosystems is unquantifiable, but will undoubtedly be staggering.

industry. The concentration of nitrates in drinking water has been steadily increasing over the years, and local water management organizations have been hard-pressed to keep these contaminant levels below government standards. Nitrates in drinking water have been linked to "Blue Baby Syndrome," several forms of cancer, goiter, spontaneous abortion and birth defects.

When you consider ethanol from the perspective of energy production, emissions, fuel efficiency and environmental impact, it is truly not the "green" fuel alternative the government proclaims it to be. THE ONLY "GREEN" IN ETHANOL COMES FROM THE HUGE AMOUNT OF MONEY WE AS A COUNTRY ARE INVESTING IN IT AND THE POWER THAT THIS "CASH-GREEN" IS GIVING TO THE AGRICULTURE INDUSTRY.

The Cost of Corn-Based Ethanol

An analysis conducted by David Pimentel, professor of ecology and agriculture at Cornell University and Tad Patzek, professor of civil and environmental engineering at the University of California Berkley, analyzed the ratio of energy input and output for ethanol. They looked at all ethanol production costs, including the costs of pesticides and fertilizers needed to grow the crops, the running of farm machinery and irrigation, the grounding and transporting of the crops, and the fermenting and distilling of ethanol from the water mix.

Their findings were as follows:

- Corn requires **29** PERCENT MORE HYDROCARBON ENERGY than the fuel it produces.
- Switch grass (a popular corn ethanol alternative) requires **45** PERCENT MORE HYDROCARBON ENERGY THAN IT PRODUCES.
- Wood biomass REQUIRES **57** PERCENT MORE HYDROCARBON ENERGY than it can produce.
- Soybean fuel used to create BIO-DIESEL REQUIRES **27** PERCENT MORE HYDROCARBON FUEL than it can produce.
- Sunflower plants require **118** PERCENT MORE HYDROCARBON FUEL in its production than it can in return.

What the analysis did not factor in was the additional cost in federal and state subsidies that are passed on to consumers in the form of additional taxes. Professor Pimentel was quoted as saying, "THE GOVERNMENT SPENDS MORE THAN **3** BILLION DOLLARS A YEAR TO SUBSIDIZE ETHANOL PRODUCTION WHEN IT DOES NOT PROVIDE A NET ENERGY BALANCE OR GAIN. It is not a renewable energy source or economic fuel! Further, its production and use contribute to air, water and soil pollution and global warming."

Stopping the Elephant that is Corn-Based Ethanol

Why does the government continue to push corn ethanol? Knowing what we know now, continuing to pursue corn-based ethanol as a legitimate biofuel alternative seems ludicrous. DOES THE GOVERNMENT KNOW ABOUT THE ISSUES WITH CORN-BASED ETHANOL? ABSOLUTELY! THE RESEARCH WE HAVE GATHERED REGARDING ETHANOL WAS DELIBERATELY DRAWN PRIMARILY FROM GOVERNMENT AGENCY STUDIES (SEE CHAPTER 8 ENDNOTES). OUR GOVERNMENT OFFICIALS KNOW THAT CORN-BASED ETHANOL WILL NEVER BE ANYTHING BUT AN EXERCISE IN MASSIVE GOVERNMENT SPENDING WITHOUT REAL PAYOFF. Yet, the push continues. The example of ethanol is just one of many issues where the government reveals its lack of Relational Intelligence®. The government simply does not understand the many unintended consequences from subsidizing ethanol... or... does it? THINK ABOUT IT!

FOOD OR FUEL

As more and more corn is being dedicated to ethanol production, the price of corn is skyrocketing and with it, **THE PRICE OF FOOD**. Between April 2007 and April 2008, the price of corn rose from 3.39 dollars per bushel to 5.15 dollars per bushel. Not only does it cost more for us to purchase our corn-on the-cob for Fourth of July barbeques, but the whole meal costs us more. Over the last year, the price of eggs has gone up 35 percent, chicken 10 percent, beef 8 percent and white bread 16 percent.

This year, we are expected to convert 3.53 billion bushels of corn into ethanol. That amount of corn could provide 104 million people with 2,000 calories every day for a year. While no one might want to eat that much corn, it is easy to see how the corn that the government is dedicating to fuel production might be better used to feed the nation's and the world's hungry.

IN NOVEMBER OF 2009, HUNGER IN THE UNITED STATES CLIMBED TO A 14 YEAR HIGH. THE AGRICULTURE DEPARTMENT REPORTED THAT 17 MILLION AMERICAN HOUSEHOLDS "HAD DIFFICULTY PUTTING ENOUGH FOOD ON THE TABLE AT TIMES DURING THE YEAR." Vicki Escarra, president of Feeding American, a nonprofit organization with over 200 food banks nationally, said that the Agriculture Department's numbers were probably understated. In a quote to New York Times reporter Brian Knowlston, Ms. Escarra states, "There are likely many more people struggling with hunger than this report states." She added, "National socioeconomic indicators, including the escalating unemployment rate and the number of working poor, lead us to believe that the number of people facing hunger will continue to rise significantly over coming years." Add to this that we can expect to see farmers switch their fields from soybeans and wheat (two other major food sources), to corn so that they too can reap the rewards of ethanol-boosted corn prices. We will see food prices continue to rise.

AS A RESULT IN SURGING FEED COSTS LINKED TO THE DEMANDS FOR MORE ETHANOL, MEAT PRICES IN THE UNITED STATES ARE RISING TO RECORD HIGHS IN 2010. WHOLESALE PORK JUMPED AS MUCH AS 25 PERCENT IN JUST ONE MONTH TO 90.68 CENTS A POUND AND BEEF IS UP 22 PERCENT TO 1.69 DOLLARS A POUND. IN MARCH 2010, HE PRICE OF CHICKEN WAS THE HIGHEST IT HAD BEEN IN ALMOST TWO YEARS.

Some people are starting to realize what the priority for ethanol could mean to the everyday consumer. Texas Governor Rick Perry became the first governor to ask the federal government to cut the 2007 ethanol mandate in half. Jean Zielger, former united National Special Rapporteur on the Right to Food, called ethanol and other bio fuels "a crime against humanity."

Not only are we as Americans paying higher prices for food, corn-based ethanol is affecting food prices throughout the world. The U.S. supplies 65 percent of corn exports across the globe. As we dedicate more of our harvest to ethanol, more people are going hungry. For example, there is a continuing crisis in Mexico over the rising cost of corn. Tortillas, a main staple for most Mexicans, made from corn, have become a prohibitive expense. In 2006, the cost per kilo of tortillas was 6 pesos (0.55 US dollars). Just a year later, the cost had risen to an average of 10 pesos (0.91 US dollars) per kilogram, with some areas charging more than 15 pesos a kilo (1.37 US dollars).

THIS MAY NOT LIKE SEEM LIKE MUCH OF AN INCREASE UNTIL YOU FACTOR IN THAT OVER 40 MILLION MEXICANS EARN LESS THAN 5 DOLLARS A DAY. In 2007, tens of thousands of workers and farmers protested the rising cost of corn, blaming the U.S. government's push for ethanol for the rise in corn prices. The rising cost of tortillas has many turning to cheaper, less nutritious food stuffs... or just going hungry.

A WORLD BANK STUDY ESTIMATED THAT CORN PRICES "ROSE BY OVER 60 PERCENT FROM 2005 TO 2007, LARGELY BECAUSE OF THE U.S. ETHANOL PROGRAM." The International Monetary Fund estimates that the shift from food crops to biofuel production accounted for half of the recent increases in global food prices, which rose 43 percent between March 2007 and March 2008.

Food shouldn't be our only concern. Growing corn requires a massive amount of water. A 2007 study at Arizona State University found that it takes 785 gallons of water just to irrigate enough corn to produce one gallon of ethanol. Only very few people are recognizing the potential impact to our water supplies if we are to meet the government's mandate of 350 billion gallons of ethanol by 2010 – it would equate to almost 275 trillion gallons of water!

CHAPTER NINE |
BLOOD FOR OIL:
CAFE STANDARDS

Again, as a result of the man-made global warming hoax, the government has been able to perpetuate a policy almost without debate, despite the dire consequences on the American public. This time the industry targeted is the American automotive industry, and the policy comes in the guise of federally imposed **CAFE** standards (**C**orporate **A**verage **F**uel **E**conomy standards).

CAFE standards force all car companies to hit a minimum average fuel economy target across their entire fleet (cars, pickups, minivans and sport utility vehicles). That means automakers have to balance the average fuel economy of their vehicles between different models. If they produce a larger vehicle with a higher miles per gallon (mpg) rating, then that automaker will also have to produce other models with lower mpg ratings to be able to meet their CAFE standard average. THE GOVERNMENT'S INTENTION FOR SETTING CAFE STANDARDS WAS TO ENCOURAGE AUTOMAKERS TO IMPROVE THE TECHNOLOGY BY WHICH VEHICLES PROCESS FUEL, MAKING THEM MORE FUEL-EFFICIENT. The problem is, automakers took an alternative route, one that put drivers in danger. But, before we address the specific consequences of CAFE standards, let's first look at how the government was able to put them into place.

A BRIEF HISTORY OF CAFE STANDARDS

It was in the Energy Policy Conservation Act back in 1975 that CAFE standards found their beginnings. In direct response to the 1973-74 Arab oil embargo, the act was meant to double fuel economy by the 1985 model year (it was unsuccessful). Enforced by National Highway Traffic Safety Administration (NHTSA), CAFE has always been a solution searching for a problem. Is it supposed to combat global warming? Is it to reduce our reliance on foreign oil? Is it designed to reduce traffic congestion and air pollution? Can it do anything at all?

Still without a definitive answer, in December of 2007, Congress with President Bush signing off, INCREASED the standards by approximately 40 percent by 2020 to a fleet wide average of 35 miles per gallon!   At the time, the new standards went into effect, the EPA had rated over 1,100 vehicle models for gas mileage. Guess how many could meet the new standards. About 20 to 25 percent of the models? Maybe only 10 to 15 percent of the models? Absolutely not. Only two cars – the Toyota Prius and the Honda Civic Hybrid. TWO CARS OUT OF MORE THAN 1,100. As auto makers were struggling about how in the world they could hit the 35 mile average by 2020, NEWLY ELECTED PRESIDENT OBAMA ANNOUNCED HE EXPECTED AUTO MAKERS TO MEET THE NEW CAFE STANDARD FOUR YEARS SOONER IN 2016!

In an even more troubling demonstration of poor Relational Intelligence®, POLLS SHOW THAT BETWEEN 78 AND 92 PERCENT OF THE PUBLIC SUPPORT CAFE STANDARDS! On the surface, this makes sense. Who does not want their cars to get more miles to the gallon? So, why are CAFE standards such a bad thing? Isn't it advantageous for the American people that the government require auto-makers to produce more fuel-efficient cars? The answer would be "Yes" if the cost both to American drivers and in human life weren't so high.

THE HIDDEN EXPENSE OF CAFE STANDARDS

As with so many government regulations, one of the major consequences of CAFE standards is that it makes cars more expensive to build. Who bears this cost – consumers, of course! The purported purpose behind CAFE standards is to reduce the amount of gasoline consumed by American drivers. The government could just put a higher tax on gas (as is done across Europe), but Congress does not want to tax gasoline because taxes are unpopular.   So, instead of taxing gasoline where people would see the government's manipulation as what it is, CAFE standards are put into place where voters cannot assess the costs directly. Despite President Obama's many calls for transparency in government, CAFE standards hide the costs of the regulation.

Instead, they impose restrictions of manufacturers who in turn, pass the costs back down to the American driver. One unintended effect is that it encourages lower-income motorists to hold on to their older gas guzzling cars, as new, more fuel-efficient models become more expensive. And poor people will be the most likely to get hurt under President Obama's new regulations.   University of California (Santa Barbara) economics professor, Stephen DeCanio,

RQ Insight

The Obama administration says the new CAFE standards will add on an average of only **1,300 DOLLARS PER CAR**.

However, Bob Lutz, former vice president of General Motors, estimates the cost of up to **6,000 DOLLARS PER VEHICLE**.

in a recent telephone conversation declared, "CAFE standards are regressive. They put an undue burden on those who are low-income, who will buy cars that are smaller and less safe. Speaking as someone who is in favor of reducing greenhouse gas emissions, CAFE is not the way to go."

CAFE's Impact on Human Life

In order to try and meet CAFE standards, automakers have not made the great strides in technology expected when CAFE first came into being. Rather, automakers have opted to simply make cars LIGHTER. It is a simple equation: heavy cars need more fuel to power them and lighter cars use less fuel. **THE PROBLEM IS LIGHTER CARS ARE ALSO LESS SAFE.** In a car crash, the physics of momentum means that a heavier object simply has more force than a lighter object. So having a light, more fuel efficient car might sound like a good idea, but you pit a Prius against an eighteen-wheeler (or strong tree) and you decide which one you'd want to be behind the wheel of during a crash.

The Department of Transportation's National Highway Traffic Safety Administration (NHTSA) studies the relationships of vehicle weight to fatality and injury risk and found the following:

- There is a 1.1 percent increase in fatalities per 100 pound decrease in vehicle weight.

- There is a 1.6 percent increase in serious or moderate injuries per 100 pound decrease in vehicle weight.

- Between 1975 and 1985 while fuel efficiency did double as the weight of many cars decreased, **NHTSA DID CONCLUDE THAT THE DOWNSIZING RESULTED IN UP TO 2,000 ADDITIONAL DEATHS AND 20,000 ADDITIONAL SERIOUS OR MODERATE INJURIES PER YEAR!**

- The study concludes… "The Office of Technology Assessment of the United States Congress, The National Safety Council, the Brookings Institution, the Insurance Institute for Highway Safety, the General Motors Research Laboratories and the National Academy of Sciences all agreed that reductions in the size and weight of passenger cars pose a safety threat."

RQ Insight

Congress has the audacity to investigate Toyota Motor Corporation for roughly 20 deaths over a 10 year time horizon.

Meanwhile, **Congress is directly responsible for enacting legislations that has KILLED TENS OF THOUSANDS of Americans**.

Who is investigating Congress?

Where is the outrage from the media? From taxpayers?

⌐ THINK.

In another 2006 report by Ryan Bilas of the National Center for Public Policy Research, several studies demonstrated the cost in human lives due to CAFE standards:

- A 1989 Harvard-Brookings study estimated that CAFE has resulted in a 500 pound weight reduction on the average car.

- Passengers in smaller, lighter cars die at a rate 12 times that of people driving larger, heavier cars.

- A 1999 USA TODAY ANALYSIS OF CRASH DATA FOUND THAT SINCE CAFE WENT INTO EFFECT IN 1978, 46,000 PEOPLE DIED IN CRASHES THEY OTHERWISE WOULD HAVE SURVIVED! THAT EQUATES TO ROUGHLY 7,700 DEATHS FOR EVERY MILE PER GALLON GAINED IN FUEL ECONOMY STANDARDS!

CAFE standards are killing thousands of people. While man-made global warming activists stridently call for us to save the polar bears and penguins, the policies they endorse are making it more deadly to take to the roads. Where is the public outrage about this horrific lack of RELATIONAL INTELLIGENCE® on the part of our government? Why aren't we bombarded by the media with headlines about how, in a pointless effort to reduce carbon emissions with the illusionary benefit of affecting global temperatures, more people have to be injured and die in unsafe cars? The silent persistence of CAFE standards is staggering in terms of how little RELATIONAL INTELLIGENCE® is at play within our government and those in our country who support these practices.

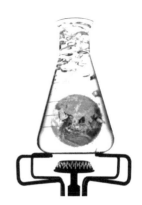

CHAPTER TEN |
CAP & TRADE:
THE REAL STORY

Not sure that ethanol will sufficiently reduce carbon emissions, our government has yet another scheme to reduce CO_2. As part of the global effort to reduce CO_2 emissions, the United States Congress is in the process of attempting to pass an incredibly expensive, economically unsound and environmentally futile piece of legislation known as the CO_2 emission cap-and-trade program, (also known as either the Waxman-Markey climate change bill or, more recently, the Kerry-Boxer bill). This bill is basically a maneuver on the part of our government to take control of the energy industry and legitimize a huge new source of federal revenue through what is basically an energy tax. REMEMBER CO_2 IS **3.62** PERCENT OF ALL GREENHOUSE GASSES AND ONLY **0.117** PERCENT OF ALL GREENHOUSE GASES IS MAN-MADE CO_2. BUT, THE RELATIONALLY AWARE REALIZE THAT THIS FACT ONLY RUNS CONTRARY TO THE GOVERNMENT'S ENERGY AGENDA.

CAP-AND-TRADE 101

The cap-and-trade program would basically work in two parts.

THE CAP: The government would be given the power to set total limits on annual man-made CO_2 emissions each year, over time gradually tightening the amount of CO_2 emissions allowed. Based on each year's cap, the government would then either sell or give emissions allowances to regulated organizations. Each allowance would entitle companies to either emit one ton of CO_2 or to produce fuel that would release one ton of CO_2 when burned.

THE TRADE: Once the government has distributed these allowances to companies, these companies would then be permitted to buy or sell these allowances amongst themselves. The companies who would be able to reduce their emissions more easily would be able to profit by selling their excess allowances to other companies who find it more difficult and expensive to meet the new regulatory emission limits.

The CO_2 cap-and-trade program is based on several other government programs already in place both within our country and internationally. Back in 1995, the U.S. passed into law a similar federal cap-and-trade program limiting the emissions of sulfur dioxide, the leading cause of acid rain. The Northeast region of the United States already has a cap-and-trade program for CO_2 emissions in place, and several other states are considering similar programs. As part of the initial phase of the Kyoto protocol, THE EUROPEAN UNION ALSO HAS A CAP-AND-TRADE PROGRAM FOR CO_2 EMISSIONS ALREADY IN PLACE (WHICH, BY THE WAY, IS FAILING MISERABLY).

Comparing Carbon Cap & Trade Costs
Figures are adjusted for inflation

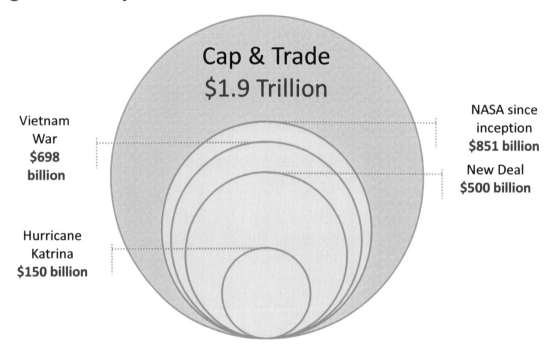

Cap & Trade
$1.9 Trillion

Vietnam War
$698 billion

Hurricane Katrina
$150 billion

NASA since inception
$851 billion

New Deal
$500 billion

Source: "Global Warming Legislation vs. Largest Government Projects in History," The Foundry Blog, April 2, 2009, Heritage Foundation. http://blog.heritage.org/2009/04/02/global-warming-legislation-vs-largest-government-projects-in-history/

The purpose behind the cap-and-trade approach is to allow companies more flexibility in how they meet government emissions standards versus having the government specify exactly how much each industry could emit and what technologies they would have to use. The cap-and-trade program is designed to curb emissions while still giving companies options in terms of how they choose to meet government requirements. However, for the energy industry, buying allowances and/or taking steps to lower emissions to avoid the need for allowances will become a new cost of doing business.

IN EFFECT, A CAP-AND-TRADE PROGRAM WOULD CREATE A NEW COMMODITY: THE RIGHT TO EMIT CARBON DIOXIDE FOR A PRICE! This right would be controlled by our government and utilized to take control of our nation's energy industry to the detriment of consumers and businesses alike. It is estimated that cap & trade would become a 10 trillion dollar commodities market. Compare this to the fact that the New York Stock Exchange is currently worth between 19 and 21 trillion dollars; you get some idea of the huge impact cap & trade could have on our economy.

Under the cap-and-trade program, it would be naïve to assume that the regulated companies would absorb the costs of the allowances. Rather, they would pass these costs down to consumers. ENERGY PRICE INCREASES AS A RESULT OF THE CARBON DIOXIDE CAP-AND-TRADE PROGRAM ARE INEVITABLE AND FOR LOWER-INCOME HOUSEHOLDS, POTENTIALLY PROHIBITIVE.

In his book, **The Real Global Warming Disaster**, Christopher Booker estimates that carbon permits traded in global exchanges such as the European Union Greenhouse Gas Emission Tradition System (EU-ETS), now worth an estimated 126 billion dollars, will soon be valued in the trillions. This will make "carbon the most valuable traded commodity in the world," outpacing even oil. Booker writes:

> *Forget big oil! The new world power is Big Carbon. Truly it has been a miracle of our time that they have managed to transform carbon dioxide, a gas upon which all life on earth depends, into a 'pollutant,' worth more than diamonds, let alone oil.*

A write up by Jerome Corsi in *Red Alert*, January 2010, states THE UNDERLYING AGENDA OF GLOBAL WARMING CLIMATE HYSTERIA IS NOT TO SAVE THE PLANET, BUT TO PROVIDE A VEHICLE WHERE PROMINENT ENTHUSIASTS OF GLOBAL WARMING, SUCH AS AL GORE AND U.N. CLIMATE CHIEF, RAJENDRA PACHAURI, CAN GET RICH BUYING AND SELLING CARBON CREDITS TO THE DETRIMENT OF U.S. ECONOMY AND THE U.S. MIDDLE CLASS.

RQ Insight

In January 2008, then presidential candidate, **BARACK OBAMA**, stated in an interview in the San Francisco Chronicle that, **"ELECTRICITY RATES WOULD NECESSARILY SKYROCKET"** under his cap-and-trade program.

THE HIGH COST OF CAP-AND-TRADE – ESPECIALLY FOR LOWER-INCOME HOUSEHOLDS

The Bureau of Labor Statistics shows that by far, lower-income households spend a much higher percentage on energy-intensive items than higher-income households: APPROXIMATELY FIVE TIMES AS MUCH (see table below).

2007 AVERAGE ANNUAL HOUSEHOLD EXPENDITURES ON ENERGY-INTENSIVE ITEMS BY INCOME QUINTILE

	Quintile					All Households
	Lowest	Second	Middle	Fourth	Highest	
Utility Expenditures	$1,203	$1,596	$1,840	$2,181	$2,847	$1,934
Gasoline Expenditures	$1,046	$1,768	$2,418	$2,988	$3,696	$2,384
Total Spending on Energy-Intensive Items	**$2,249**	**$3,364**	$4,258	$5,169	$6,543	$4,318
Total as a Percentage of Income	**21.4**	**12.2**	9.2	7.1	4.1	6.8

Source: Congressional Budget Office based on data from Bureau of Labor Statistics, Consumer Expenditure Survey, 2007. Available at http://www.bis.gov/cex/2007/Standard/quintile.pdf

The increase in energy prices as a result of the cap-and-trade program for carbon dioxide would exacerbate this problem dramatically. While the Environmental Protection Agency predicted that the cap-and-trade program would cost households an additional 140 dollars a year, the Heritage Foundation did its own analysis and found that the EPA failed to account for many critical economic factors when coming up with their cost numbers. ACCORDING TO THE HERITAGE FOUNDATION, THE REAL IMPACT OF THE CAP-AND-TRADE PROGRAM WOULD BE AN INCREASE OF 1,288 DOLLARS PER HOUSEHOLD BY 2020. ADJUSTED TO A HOUSEHOLD SIZE FOR A FAMILY OF FOUR, THAT COST RISES TO OVER 1,900 DOLLARS ANNUALLY. BY 2035, A FAMILY OF FOUR WOULD BE FACING AN INCREASE OF 6,800 DOLLARS IN THEIR ENERGY COSTS!

This only accounts for energy-intensive items such as natural gas, electricity, fuel oil, other heating fuels, gasoline and motor oil. While these items will most likely see the greatest increase in price, costs for many other items will also inevitably rise as a result of the cap-and-trade program, including the cost of food. This will place even more of a burden on lower-income households as they decide how to apportion their monthly expenditures: should they buy the higher priced food they need to feed their family, pay their electric bill to keep their family warm, or fill their gas tanks so they can keep going to work, all the while forgoing things like health care, school supplies and even haircuts? Within the lower-income group, the hardest hit will be families with young children and the elderly. EVEN THE CONGRESSIONAL BUDGET OFFICE AFFIRMS THAT THE PRICE INCREASES (AS A PERCENTAGE OF INCOME) FOR ITEMS OTHER THAN GASOLINE AND OTHER FUELS WOULD ACCOUNT FOR APPROXIMATELY 40 PERCENT OF THE TOTAL PRICE INCREASE FOR HOUSEHOLDS AS A DIRECT RESULT OF THE CAP-AND-TRADE PROGRAM.

In addition, many Americans may also find their jobs become victim to the cap-and-trade program. Corporations will be squeezed on two sides. On the one side, corporations will need to pay for emissions allowances, as well as invest in emission-reducing technologies. On the other side, they will watch as consumer demand decreases as a result of rising energy prices. Troubled investors in the energy industry will lose confidence as the value of their stocks decline. Companies will start cost cutting (i.e., layoffs) and many smaller firms will close their doors entirely as they will be unable to afford the allowances or make the necessary upgrades to reduce the carbon dioxide emissions.

Outside of the energy industry, the National Federation of Independent Businesses states the cost of fuel (natural gas, propane, gasoline or diesel) ranks as the second greatest challenge for small business owners. AS THE COST OF FUEL INCREASES, AS IT INEVITABLY WILL UNDER THE CAP-AND-TRADE PROGRAM, SMALL BUSINESSES WILL BE PUT OUT OF BUSINESS. THE TRUCKING INDUSTRY, WHO HAULS 11 BILLION TONS OF FREIGHT EVERY DAY FROM ONE END OF THE NATION TO THE OTHER AND EVERYWHERE IN-BETWEEN, WILL BE ESPECIALLY HARD HIT BY INCREASED ENERGY COSTS CAUSING THE PRICES OF EVERYTHING THEY SHIP TO INCREASE, AS WELL. The same can be said for farmers who already battle low profit margins. Any increase in their operating costs almost immediately translates to consumers but even still, it is estimated that those farmers who survive will face an increase in production costs from 5 billion dollars a year to 13 billion dollars a year. IN THE END, THREE SEPARATE STUDIES HAVE SHOWN THAT THE CAP-AND-TRADE PROGRAM WILL COST MORE THAN TWO MILLION AMERICAN JOBS!

Another report from Senators Hutchison (R-Texas) and Bond (R-Missouri), showed that between 2010 and 2035, motorists, workers and businesses would pay 2 trillion dollars more for gasoline and 1.3 trillion more in diesel fuel. Airline passengers will be charged 330 billion dollars more to offset the increased price in jet fuel.

FINALLY, THE WORST PART OF THE CARBON DIOXIDE CAP-AND-TRADE PROGRAM IS THAT ALL OF THESE CONSEQUENCES WILL BE REALIZED EXCEPT ONE: WE WILL IN NO SIGNIFICANT WAY CHANGE THE AMOUNT OF MAN-MADE CARBON DIOXIDE RELEASED INTO THE ATMOSPHERE WHICH, IN COMPARISON TO THE AMOUNT OF CO_2 RELEASED BY OUR OCEANS, IS TOTALLY INSIGNIFICANT. The caps, the allowances, the increased costs and hardships especially lower-income American's will face will make absolutely no difference to our climate, environment or planet. The economic, political and social consequences of the cap-and-trade bill, however, will be devastating.

ENRON AND CAP & TRADE

In his book, **Air Con: The Seriously Inconvenient Truth About Global Warming**, Ian Wishart, writes about how the 1990 Clean Air Act amendments authorized the Environmental Protection Agency to put a cap on how much pollutant the operator of a fossil-fuelled plant was allowed to emit. In the early 1990's, Enron had helped establish the market for, and became the major trader in, EPA's 20 billion dollar per year sulfur dioxide cap-and-trade program, the forerunner of today's proposed carbon credit trade. This commodity exchange of emission allowances caused Enron's stock to rapidly rise.

Then came the inevitable questions, what next? How about a carbon dioxide cap-and-trade program? The problem was that CO_2 is not a pollutant, and therefore the EPA had no authority to cap its emission. Al Gore took office in 1993 and almost immediately became infatuated with the idea of an international environmental regulatory regime. He led the U.S. initiative to review new projects around the world and issue 'credits' of so many tons of annual CO_2 emission reduction.

Among the new appointees to the Clinton administration was former Colorado Democrat senator Tim Wirth, the new Undersecretary of State for Global Affairs. WIRTH WORKED CLOSELY WITH GORE ON CLIMATE AND ENVIRONMENTAL ISSUES, AND ENRON BOSS KEN LAY CULTIVATED A RELATIONSHIP WITH WIRTH TO PUSH THE IDEA OF SOME KIND OF MARKET FOR CARBON CREDITS.

"UNDER LAW, A TRADABLE SYSTEM WAS REQUIRED, WHICH WAS EXACTLY WHAT ENRON ALSO WANTED BECAUSE THEY WERE ALREADY TRADING POLLUTANT CREDITS," says Ken Ring. "Hence Enron vigorously lobbied Clinton and Congress, seeking EPA regulatory authority over CO_2. From 1994 to 1996, the Enron Foundation contributed nearly 1 million dollars to the Nature Conservancy, whose Climate Change Project promotes global warming theories. Enron philanthropists lavished almost 1.5 million dollars on environmental groups that support international energy control to "reduce" global warming.

"EXECUTIVES AT ENRON WORKED CLOSELY WITH THE CLINTON ADMINISTRATION TO HELP CREATE A SCAREMONGERING CLIMATE SCIENCE ENVIRONMENT BECAUSE THE COMPANY BELIEVED THE TREATY COULD PROVIDE IT WITH A MONSTROUS FINANCIAL WINDFALL. The plan was that once the problem was in place, the solution would be trotted out," writes Ring.

Among the bedfellows Enron roped into the cause were the Heinz Foundation and the Pew Center, whose climate change divisions heavily hyped the global warming paranoia. Enron pumped serious money into groups like Pew, and stooped to some dirty tricks in the process. A 1998 letter signed by Enron's then-CEO, Ken Lay, begged "President Clinton, in essence, to harm the reputations and credibility of scientists who argued that global warming was an overblown issue. Apparently they were standing in Enron's way," writes the Cato Institute's Patrick J. Michaels.

"THE LETTER, DATED SEPT 1, ASKED THE PRESIDENT TO SHUT OFF THE PUBLIC SCIENTIFIC DEBATE ON GLOBAL WARMING, WHICH CONTINUES TO THIS DATE. IN PARTICULAR, IT REQUESTED CLINTON TO 'MODERATE THE POLITICAL ASPECTS OF THIS DISCUSSION BY APPOINTING A BIPARTISAN 'BLUE RIBBON COMMISSION'," continues Michaels.

The purpose of this commission was clear: high-level trashing of dissident scientists. Setting up a panel to do this is simple – just look at the latest issue of **Scientific America**, where four attack dogs were called out to chew up poor Bjorn Lomberg. He had the audacity to publish a book, **Cool It**, demonstrating man-made global warming is overblown.

Because of the arcane nature of science, it's easy to trash scientists. Imagine a 1940 congressional hearing to discredit Einstein. 'This man actually believes the faster you drive, the slower your watch runs. Mr. Einstein, then why weren't you here yesterday?' The public, listening on radio, immediately concludes this Princeton weirdo is just another academic egghead. End of reputation.

The proposed commission was billed as an 'education effort' that would lead to 'subsequent policy action', which the letter itself recommended. These included a directive to 'establish the rules for crediting early, voluntary emissions reductions [of carbon dioxide].' And who was going to sell these credits? Enron, of course.

ENRON POURED HUGE AMOUNTS OF MONEY INTO GREASING THE RIGHT POLITICAL PALMS. INTERNAL ENRON MEMORANDA DISCLOSE SOME OF THESE ACTIVITIES, SUCH AS AN AUGUST 4, 1997 MEETING AT THE WHITEHOUSE WITH CLINTON AND GORE TO DRUM OUT AN APPROACH TO THE UPCOMING KYOTO CONFERENCE THAT DECEMBER.

In an August 1997 memo by Mr. Lay to all Enron employees, THE CHAIRMAN SAID MR. CLINTON AND MR. GORE HAD "SOLICITED" HIS VIEW ON HOW TO ADDRESS THE ISSUE OF GLOBAL WARMING "IN ADVANCE OF A CLIMATE TREATY TO BE NEGOTIATED AT AN INTERNATIONAL CONFERENCE." That memo said MR. CLINTON agreed a market-based solution, such as EMISSIONS TRADING, WAS THE ANSWER TO REDUCING CARBON DIOXIDE IN THE ATMOSPHERE.

Ken Lay would later give key staff a briefing on his Washington sojourn, noting an internal Enron memo that "the Kyoto agreement if implemented, would 'do more to promote Enron's business than almost any other regulatory initiative outside of restructuring the energy and natural gas industries in Europe and the United States."

Tim Wirth was doing his bit, having been delegated the task as lead negotiator for the US in Kyoto, and when Vice President Al Gore signed off Kyoto in December 1997, Enron thought all its Christmases had come at once.

"This agreement will be good for Enron stock!!" exclaimed one of Enron's men in Kyoto, who in the same memo to head office peppered the main points of the newly-agreed Kyoto Protocol with phrases like, "We won," "Another victory for us," and "Exactly what I have been lobbying for."

But alas, it wasn't meant to be. Despite pouring almost 5 million dollars into political campaign donations for both Democrats and Republicans, Enron's dreams of the U.S. ratifying Kyoto were shattered when the Clinton administration realized it couldn't get the numbers to pass the law.

The reason was simple: ADOPTING KYOTO WOULD RAISE FUEL PRICES BY MORE THAN 50 PERCENT, AND ELECTRICITY PRICES WOULD ALMOST DOUBLE. THE COST TO THE US ECONOMY ANNUALLY WAS ESTIMATED AT AS MUCH AS 400 BILLION DOLLARS, YET THE GAINS ACCORDING TO CLINTON'S SCIENCE ADVISERS WOULD BE NEGLIGIBLE, WITH ALMOST NO REDUCTION IN WORLD TEMPERATURE BY 2050.

FOLLOW THE MONEY: AL GORE & CO. PROFIT FROM THEIR OWN CAUSE

AL GORE REPORTEDLY STANDS TO BENEFIT GREATLY FROM PROPOSED "CAP-AND-TRADE" AND OTHER LEGISLATION — AND POSSIBLY BECOME THE FIRST "CLIMATE BILLIONAIRE." It seems the former vice president is playing both sides of the fence on the energy front. He has made millions of dollars in private energy ventures first in his role as partner in Kleiner, Perkins, Caufield & Byers, a venture capital firm that invests in technology to address global warming. Also, through his London-based startup company called Generation Investment Management (GIM), founded with three former bigwigs from Goldman Sachs Asset Management, David Blood, Mark Ferguson and Peter Harris. Their business? Investing in carbon offsets.

ACCORDING TO THE NEW YORK TIMES, AL GORE WILL PROFIT SIGNIFICANTLY FROM THE GOVERNMENT'S ENERGY POLICIES FOR WHICH HE IS LOBBYING. Through GIM, he stands to reap huge profits from cap-and-trade legislation that would mandate carbon trading. The Competitive Enterprise Institute, a libertarian think tank, stated in a press release, "What we discover in looking at the policies that Mr. Gore advocated… is that they will make him and his friends extremely wealthy at the expense of consumers, who will be stuck with skyrocketing energy prices." Furthermore, GIM won't allow lower and middle income Americans the opportunity to benefit from the legislation. ACCORDING TO A GIM PRESS RELEASE, ONLY "INSTITUTIONAL INVESTORS" AND "SELECT HIGH NET WORTH INDIVIDUALS" CAN INVEST WITH GIM.

As for Gore's partners, they stem from Goldman Sachs, who also has its hands in the carbon allowance cookie jar. Goldman Sachs holds 11.75 percent interest in Climate Exchange PLC, which, in turn owns the Chicago Climate Exchange, the exchange where corporations will buy, sell, and trade the government's carbon credits. Like all commodity exchanges, the Chicago Climate Exchange charges a commission on all trades made on the exchange. IF THE CAP-AND-TRADE BILL PASSES, CARBON TRADERS AND GOLDMAN SACHS WILL MAKE MILLIONS, POSSIBLY BILLIONS, FROM COMMISSIONS ON CARBON TRADING.

It should be no surprise then that Goldman Sachs' political action committee donated nearly one million dollars to Barack Obama's presidential campaign. Furthermore, Goldman Sachs employees gave 687,605 dollars to the Obama campaign. Interestingly, Goldman Sachs requires employees to submit all political donations for review in order for Goldman Sachs to determine, "if they are consistent with our [organization's] policies."

In early 2010, Goldman Sachs has come under congressional investigation for a variety of unsavory dealings. But, while senators froth over Goldman Sachs and derivatives, a climate trading scheme being run out of the Chicago Climate Exchange would make Bernie Madoff blush. Its trail leads to the White House.

Lost in the recent headlines was Al Gore's appearance in Denver at the annual meeting of the Council of Foundations, an association of the nation's philanthropic leaders. "Time's running out [on climate change]," Gore told them. "We have to get our act together. You have a unique role in getting our act together."

Gore was right that foundations will play a key role in keeping the climate scam alive as evidence of outright climate fraud grows, just as they were critical in the beginning when the Joyce Foundation in 2000 and 2001 provided the seed money to start the Chicago Climate Exchange. IT STARTED TRADING IN 2003, AND WHAT IT TRADES IS, ESSENTIALLY, AIR. MORE SPECIFICALLY PERHAPS, HOT AIR.

The Chicago Climate Exchange (CCX) advertises itself as "North America's only cap-and-trade system for all six greenhouse gases, with global affiliates and projects worldwide." Barack Obama served on the board of the Joyce Foundation from 1994 to 2002 when the CCX startup grants were issued. As president, pushing cap-and-trade is one of his highest priorities. Now isn't that special?

Few Americans have heard of either entity. The Joyce Foundation was originally the financial nest egg of a widow whose family had made millions in the now out-of-favor lumber industry. After her death, the foundation was run by philanthropists who increasingly dedicated their giving to liberal causes, including gun control, environmentalism and school changes. CURRENTLY, CCX MEMBERS AGREE TO A VOLUNTARY BUT LEGALLY BINDING AGREEMENT TO REGULATE GREENHOUSE GASES. The CCX provides the mechanism in trading the very pollution permits and carbon offsets the administration's cap-and-trade proposals would impose by government mandate.

Thanks to Fox News' Glenn Beck, we have learned a lot about CCX, not the least of which is that its founder, Richard Sandor, says he knew Obama well back in the day when the Joyce Foundation awarded money to the Kellogg Graduate School of Management at Northwestern University, where Sandor was a research professor. SANDOR ESTIMATES THAT CLIMATE TRADING COULD BE "A 10 TRILLION DOLLAR MARKET." It could very well be, if cap-and-trade measures like Waxman-Markey and Kerry-Boxer are signed into law, making energy prices skyrocket, and as companies buy and sell permits to emit those six "greenhouse" gases.

So lucrative does this market appear, it attracted the attention of Al Gore's company GIM, which purchased a stake in CCX and is now the fifth-largest shareholder. Other founders include former Goldman Sachs partner David Blood, as well as Mark Ferguson and Peter Harris, also of Goldman Sachs. In 2006, CCX received a big boost when another investor bought a 10 percent stake on the prospect of making a great deal of money for itself. That investor was Goldman Sachs, now under the gun for selling financial instruments it knew were doomed to fail.

THE ACTUAL MECHANISM FOR TRADING ON THE EXCHANGE WAS PURCHASED AND PATENTED BY NONE OTHER THAN FRANKLIN RAINES, WHO WAS CEO OF FANNIE MAE AT THE TIME. Raines profited handsomely to the tune of some 90 million dollars by buying and bundling bad mortgages that led to the collapse of the American economy. His interest in climate trading is curious until one realizes cap-and-trade would make housing costlier as well.

Amazingly, none of these facts came up at Senate hearings on Goldman Sachs' activities, which may be nothing more than Ross Perot's famous "gorilla dust," meant to distract us from the real issues. The climate trading scheme being stitched together here will do more damage than Goldman Sachs, AIG and Fannie Mae combined. But it will bring power and money to its architects.

AL GORE'S PARTNER IN NOBEL PEACE CRIME

There is one more Al Gore pal who is in line for a heafty payout for his man-made global warming efforts. Who is it? THE MULTI-MILLIONAIRE INDIAN INDUSTRIAL ENGINEER, RAJENDRA K. PACHAURI, WHO HAS BEEN THE CHAIR OF THE U.N. INTERGOVERNMENTAL PANEL ON CLIMATE CHANGE (IPCC) SINCE 2002. Dr. Pachauri shared the Nobel Peace Prize with Al Gore in 2007 for leading the global warming charge. Since that time, however, the truth about Dr. Pachauri has come out. Through his extensive international business relationships, it has been shown that PACHAURI STANDS TO MAKE HUGE PROFITS FROM GLOBAL WARMING LEGISLATION. Pachauri has links to organizations who cash in on EU carbon credits to others who extract and use carbon dioxide for the propagation of a micro-algae scheme.

IN ADDITION, DR. PACHAURI WAS RECENTLY FORCED TO ADMIT THAT A PREDICTION HE MADE IN 2007 THAT THE HIMALAYAN GLACIERS WERE "VERY LIKELY" TO MELT BY 2035 HAD ABSOLUTELY NO BASIS IN FACT. Amid calls for his resignation, Dr. Pachauri deflected accountability. He told the London Times that, "I know a lot of climate skeptics are after my blood, but I am in no mood to oblige them. It was the collective failure by a number of people. I need to consider what action to take, but that will take several weeks. It's best to think with a cool head, rather than shoot from the hip." Well, sadly for Dr. Pachauri, it's too late for that. All of the "shoot from the hip" reports from his organization pushing false data about global warming have already taken their toll and the damage has been done. But, the man once heralded as the "world's leading climate scientist" is now being tagged by the global media as a "controversial former railroad engineer" and "lobbyist." His time in his U.N. position may be limited.

CAP & TRADE BACK UP PLAN

In December of 2009, the Environmental Protection Agency, acting under the authority of the Clean Air Act, took steps to control carbon emissions blamed for global warming from power plants, factories and refineries without waiting for Congress to act on cap-and-trade. The EPA ruled that GREENHOUSE GASES SUCH AS CARBON DIOXIDE ENDANGER HUMAN HEALTH under the Clean Air Act, DESPITE THE FACT HUMAN BEINGS EXHALE CARBON DIOXIDE THAT TREES AND OTHER PLANTS ABSORB. When the head of the EPA was asked what the "endangerment finding" was based on, THE ANSWER WAS THE IPCC. Really? With all of the false data coming out of the IPCC (the "hockey stick" charts being just one example), CONGRESS NEEDS TO CHALLENGE THE EPA'S "ENDANGERMENT FINDING."

The EPA decision opened the door for the Obama administration to impose restriction on the use of carbon-based fuels in the United States, even if Congress never passes the administration's proposed cap and trade legislation. The Associated Press reported that the EPA would require all individual industrial plants that emit 25,000 tons of greenhouse gases a year or more to install technology to improve energy efficiency whenever a facility is changed or built. The EPA has also delayed 79 coal-mining permits in four states, arguing the planned coal mining operations would cause significant damage to water quality and the environment under the specifications of the Clean Water Act.

HOAX

part four | THE RQ OF MAN-MADE GLOBAL WARMING

In the third part of this book, we have shown in detail how the U.S. government has leveraged public support of man-made global warming to institute various policies that will not only threaten American livelihoods, but their very lives. This fourth and final part of the book will feature how we as individuals and as a country can exhibit more Relational Intelligence® about man-made global warming (and with other issues, as well.) First, we will take a serious look at the very real, safe and cost-effective energy alternative presented by nuclear power, and how a very dated perspective on this energy source has colored its true potential.

CHAPTER ELEVEN |

IF YOU ARE SERIOUS ABOUT REDUCING CO$_2$, EMBRACE NUCLEAR POWER

HOPEFULLY BY THIS POINT, YOU HAVE BECOME SO RELATIONALLY INTELLIGENT ABOUT MAN-MADE GLOBAL WARMING THAT YOU SEE THE CAUSE FOR THE HOAX THAT IT IS. However, there are other reasons why our energy policies in the U.S. need to be addressed. As long as we are continually forced to import oil to meet our ever-growing energy needs, our nation's economic, industrial and political strength will be at the mercy of forces beyond our control. It is only through energy independence that we will be able to build upon and further our nation's legacy. We are in a position to not only end our dependence on foreign oil, but become an exporter of energy to the rest of the world. Yet, the United States continues to throw away over 300 billion dollars each year to import foreign oil and gas that we import primarily from the Middle East and continues to emit CO$_2$.

Why? Because OUR GOVERNMENT HAS OUR DOMESTIC ENERGY INDUSTRY COMPLETELY HAMSTRUNG. The United States government does not produce energy. Private industry does and our government has made the energy business a tough one, indeed. Unlike many other countries where energy production has thrived, the United States government taxes, regulates and legislates the energy industry into a weakened condition. If that wasn't enough, our government also subsidizes energy technologies that are inferior and incapable of meeting even a minor portion of our energy needs. As a result, energy independence seems to be an unattainable goal.

Our only hope is that we get realistic about our energy future. There are only three ways the United States can liberate itself from foreign oil and potentially become a net energy exporter.

- A. Increase our use of hydrocarbon energy
- B. Greatly increase our use of nuclear energy
- C. Both A and B

RELATIONAL INTELLIGENCE® AND DEEP WATER DRILLING

The government, the media and the public have been placing much of the blame for the Deepwater Horizon oil spill on British Petroleum (BP). But few are asking why BP was drilling more than 50 miles offshore where water was 5,000 feet deep. What the media has not reported is that in 2008, the Democratic controlled Congress passed an Energy Bill, which restricted oil drilling to beyond a 50 mile limit from our shores, a restriction proposed by House Speaker Nancy Pelosi and voted for by then Senator Barack Obama.

According to a Sept 17, 2008 Boston Globe report, voters deeply concerned about the distressed economy and high gasoline prices pressured the Democratic majority into allowing ocean drilling. Democrats had resisted Republican proposals to end a longtime ban on offshore drilling, but with the ban set to expire at the end of September and the November elections approaching, House Speaker Nancy Pelosi shifted her stance, proposing legislation that would allow drilling beyond 50 miles from shore.

House minority leader John Boehner protested that the vast majority of known offshore oil is within 50 miles of shore and would therefore still be off-limits. But, environmentalists had pressured the Democrats to keep the drilling far offshore, fearing that an accidental oil spill would foul the Gulf's shoreline.

FORCING DRILLING OFFSHORE BY 50 MILES ALSO FORCED IT INTO DEEPER WATERS. Ironically, should a spill occur, the deep waters would **MAKE A DISASTER MORE LIKELY**, not less likely because the frigid temperatures and the high water pressure would frustrate deep sea technological attempts to stop the leak.

This has been the exact case in the Deepwater Horizon spill. The depth of the water makes it extremely difficult to get the spill under control. Current technology is just not advanced enough to handle a spill of this magnitude and depth.

An applicable comparison would be if the government set new regulations that commercial aircrafts could only fly above 80,000 feet. The average top altitude that most planes fly today is between 30,000 and 40,000 feet. Airlines would be hard pressed to meet the new "80,000 feet" regulation in any cost-effective and safety-conscious way. But, that is basically what the government expected oil companies to do when they set the 50 mile limit on off-shore drilling. They not only made the drilling more challenging, but far more dangerous not only for the environment, but for drilling platform personnel (remembering the eleven men who died in the explosion and the 17 other workers who were injured).

Certainly BP should bear its share of the blame for the spill, but **CONGRESS AND PRESIDENT OBAMA ALSO DESERVE THEIR SHARE OF RESPONSIBILITY AS WELL FOR FORCING DRILLING INTO DEEPER WATERS.** Near shore drilling in Alaska as well as Mexico and China have shown that tapping underwater oil reserves can be environmentally safe as long as government doesn't push drilling beyond its current technological capacity, which is exactly what happened in the case of the Deepwater Horizon oil spill.

As now proven, there is absolutely no basis for man-made global warming. As such, our continued use of hydrocarbon fuels is an economically and environmentally sound approach for meeting our current and future energy needs. We need to "drill here and drill now... safely" before the next oil crisis – which will happen and happen soon.

Comparison of Life Cycle Emissions
Tons of CO_2 Equivalent to GWh (one billion watt-hours)

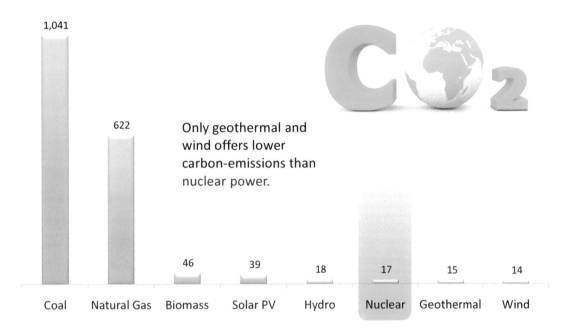

Only geothermal and wind offers lower carbon-emissions than nuclear power.

Coal	Natural Gas	Biomass	Solar PV	Hydro	Nuclear	Geothermal	Wind
1,041	622	46	39	18	17	15	14

Source: "Life-Cycle Assessment of Electricity Generation Systems and Applications for Climate Change Policy Analysis," Paul J. Meier, University of Wisconsin-Madison, August 2002.

HOWEVER, IF OUR GOVERNMENT PERSISTS IN PUSHING A REDUCTION OF UNITED STATES HYDROCARBON USE BY 90 PERCENT AND ELIMINATING 75 PERCENT OF OUR ENERGY SUPPLY, THEN OTHER SOURCES WILL HAVE TO BE FOUND… AND QUICKLY. The best option available today is NUCLEAR ENERGY. It is less expensive and more environmentally benign than hydrocarbon fuels. The only problem with nuclear energy is that it, too, has become a victim of the politics of fear where many claims of its hazardous and dangerous potential are either highly exaggerated, if not completely false.

NUCLEAR POWER IS "EMISSIONS-FREE"

Currently, nuclear power is the only technology capable of providing emissions-free energy on the scale required to significantly reduce carbon emissions. In the United States, almost 700 million metric tons of CO_2 emissions annually are avoided due to nuclear-generated electricity. Worldwide, nuclear generation reduces emissions by almost 2 billion metric tons below what they otherwise would be.

However, thanks to environmental anti-nuclear activism going back to the 1970s, building a nuclear plant takes a ridiculous amount of time. According to the Nuclear Energy Institute, building a new nuclear power plant takes 10 years from concept to operation. ONLY FOUR OF THOSE YEARS ARE NEEDED FOR ACTUAL CONSTRUCTION. The remaining six years are consumed by permit application development (two years) and decision making by the Nuclear Regulatory Commission (four years). This raises development and construction costs to the level that nuclear power is not economically competitive with forms of electricity generation that actually do emit greenhouse gases, such as coal and natural gas.

The application and approval process has been streamlined over the past decade, but more needs to be done. A potential nuclear power plant builder who has not yet decided to begin construction can file an Early Site Permit application, but it takes an average of **33** MONTHS for the Nuclear Regulatory Commission to review it. By contrast, the United Kingdom is introducing a new licensing process under which planning, application and licensing together will take no longer than **18** MONTHS. The United Kingdom's example proves that the process within our own country could be significantly reduced without sacrificing safety or construction standards.

SETTING NUCLEAR POWER FREE

There are policy changes that can significantly cut the costs of nuclear power-plant construction and make nuclear power more competitive with other generation technologies.

PUT THE INDUSTRY IN CHARGE OF FUEL CYCLE MANAGEMENT – Under the Energy Policy Act of 1982, the federal government was supposed to collect and manage spent nuclear fuel. Despite failing to do so, it continues to collect fees for that purpose. The industry should have the responsibility and ability to decide how to dispose of the fuel safely. Without an effective and agreed-upon approach to the management of nuclear waste, nuclear power is likely to remain too risky an investment.

REMOVE COMMODITY TARIFFS – Prices for vital construction materials such as steel and cement are artificially inflated by tariffs. Removing import tariffs would reduce construction costs. For example, large amounts of concrete are used in the construction of nuclear power stations, but thanks to high tariffs, the United States is experiencing a cement shortage. Cement producers such as Mexico have found that it is more profitable to send shipments to China than to the United States because of a 40 percent United States import tariff. In 2004, the Portland Cement Association, a trade group representing American and Canadian companies, found that 29 states were experiencing shortages despite the fact that virtually all United States cement plants were working around the clock, seven days a week. Lifting or reducing the tariffs would obviously benefit other areas of the economy, such as home building, making this a wide-reaching no-regrets policy.

WHY IS THIS A NO-REGRETS POLICY? – Over the next 20 years, U.S. electricity demand is expected to increase more than 45 percent. Even the most comprehensive conservation and efficiency efforts would offset less than one-fourth of this increase in demand. Not counting hydropower, the rated capacity of all renewable energy combined is less than 2 percent of total generating capacity. Furthermore, intermittent sources of electric power, such as solar and wind, require redundant power plants. Power plants fueled by coal, natural gas or nuclear fuel are the only reliable sources or baseload power (required to keep electric power flowing) and peaking power (required to meet daily spikes in demand). **NATURAL GAS AND COAL BOTH EMIT CO2 AS A BYPRODUCT OF COMBUSTION. NUCLEAR ENERGY DOES NOT.**

Absent a significant breakthrough in the capture of carbon, nuclear fuel, which emits no CO_2, is clearly preferable for electric power. Increasing nuclear power generation can supply the energy needed for continued growth while reducing future carbon emissions.

RQ Insight

Our exhaled breath contains about
4 percent CO_2. That's 40,000 parts
per million or about 100 times the
current atmospheric concentration.

If man-made global warming
enthusiasts really want to save the
world by limited CO_2 emissions...
they should all just **HOLD THEIR
BREATH**.

CHAPTER TWELVE |
A FINAL WORD ON THE MAN-MADE GLOBAL WARMING HOAX

When later generations learn about climate science, they will classify the beginning of the twenty-first century as an embarrassing chapter in the history of science. They will wonder about our time and use it as a warning of how the core values and criteria of science were allowed little by little to be forgotten, as the actual research topic of climate change turned into a political and social playground.

– Atte Korhola, Professor of Environmental Change
University of Helsinki

In 1912, Charles Dawson discovered the first of two skulls found in the Piltdown quarry in Sussex, England. The skulls were thought to be of a primitive hominid, an ancestor of man. Piltdown man, or *Eoanthropus dawsoni*, was an immediate sensation. He was the greatly anticipated "missing link" – a mixture of man and ape with the noble brow of Homo sapiens and a primitive jaw. But, as time went on, Piltdown man became a problem for the scientific community. Later finds of ancient hominids proved Piltdown man as an anomaly, a creature without a place in the human family tree. Finally, in 1953, the truth came out. Piltdown man was a **HOAX, A FOSSIL OF AN ANCIENT PEOPLE WHO NEVER EXISTED.**

How did the Piltdown hoax persist for 41 years? The hoax succeeded in large part because of the careless nature of the testing applied to it. Careful examination using methods available at the time would have immediately revealed the hoax. The failure to adequately examine the fossils went unmarked and unnoticed in large part because the hoax satisfied theoretical expectations of the time. Scientists were looking for the "missing link." The find was "expected" among scientists so they saw no need to verify if it was actually real.

Piltdown man is indicative of some very common and dangerous pitfalls in the scientific process. First, there is the danger of inadequate examination and unwillingness to challenge results that confirm the currently accepted scientific interpretation. The second is that a result, once established, tends to be uncritically accepted and relied upon without further reconsideration.

Prominent anthropologists spent years of their lives exploring the properties of what turned out to be a fake. More than five hundred articles and memoirs were written about the Piltdown finds before the hoax was exposed; all of it a wasted effort. Likewise articles in encyclopedias and sections in text books, and popular books of science were all simply wrong. PILTDOWN MAN IS A BLACK MARK ON THE SCIENCE OF HUMAN ANCESTRY THAT TOOK 41 YEARS TO EXPOSE AS A HOAX, BUT IT WILL PALE IN COMPARISON TO THE LARGER HOAX CURRENTLY BEING REVEALED; THAT OF MAN-MADE GLOBAL WARMING.

SLAYING THE DRAGON OF MAN-MADE GLOBAL WARMING

THE PRIMARY ARGUMENT OF THIS BOOK IS THAT A LACK OF RELATIONAL INTELLIGENCE® ON THE PART OF SCIENTISTS, OUR GOVERNMENT, THE MEDIA AND THE PEOPLE OF THE WORLD IS ALLOWING THE MAN-MADE GLOBAL WARMING HOAX TO PERSIST. The most significant measure of this lack of RQ is the continued belief that man is responsible for emitting far more carbon dioxide into the atmosphere than is actually the case, and that this increase in carbon dioxide is affecting global temperatures.

While this book and several others try their best to awaken the public to the truth, a surprising majority of people still believe in man-made global warming. A recent survey conducted by the Political Psychology Research Group showed that large majorities of Americans still believe the earth has been gradually warming as the result of human activity, and want the government to institute regulations to stop it.

Financed by a grant to Stanford from the National Science Foundation, 1,000 randomly selected American adults were interviewed by phone in early June 2010. When respondents were asked if they thought that the earth's temperature probably had been heating up over the last 100 years, 75 percent answered affirmatively. 75 PERCENT OF RESPONDENTS SAID THAT HUMAN BEHAVIOR WAS SUBSTANTIALLY RESPONSIBLE FOR ANY WARMING THAT HAS OCCURRED. For many issues, any such consensus about the existence of a problem quickly falls apart when the conversation turns to carrying out specific solutions that will be costly (like immigration or education). But, this is not the case with man-made global warming.

Fully 86 percent of respondents said they wanted the federal government to limit the amount of air pollution that businesses emit, and 76 percent favored government limiting business's emissions of greenhouse gases in particular. NOT A MAJORITY OF 55 OR 60 PERCENT — BUT 76 PERCENT.

While large numbers of respondents opposed taxes on electricity (78 percent) and gasoline (72 percent) to reduce consumption, 84 PERCENT FAVORED THE FEDERAL GOVERNMENT OFFERING TAX BREAKS TO ENCOURAGE UTILITIES TO MAKE MORE ELECTRICITY FROM WATER, WIND AND SOLAR POWER. The survey showed that people continue to believe the government should take action to address man-made global warming and that people continue to be unaware of the dramatic negative consequences various man-made global warming policies will incur. ONLY 18 PERCENT OF RESPONDENTS SAID THEY THOUGHT THAT POLICIES TO REDUCE GLOBAL WARMING WOULD INCREASE UNEMPLOYMENT, AND ONLY 20 PERCENT SAID THEY THOUGHT SUCH INITIATIVES WOULD HURT THE NATION'S ECONOMY.

The poll did not even touch upon other initiatives that are endangering both our economy and our lives: the continued push for corn-based ethanol production and consumption, the catastrophically expensive carbon cap-and-trade program which has already been passed by the House of Representatives, and the deadly CAFE fuel economy standards which is pushing car manufacturers to produce fleets of light, more deadly vehicles.

The poll did reveal a small recent decline in the proportion of people who believe global warming has been happening, FROM 84 PERCENT IN 2007 TO 80 PERCENT IN 2008 TO 74 PERCENT TODAY. But, statistical analysis of the survey data revealed that this decline can be attributed to perceptions of recent weather changes by the minority of Americans who are also skeptical about climate scientists due to recent scandals like "Climategate."

In terms of average earth temperature, 2008 was the coldest year since 2000. Scientists say that such year-to-year fluctuations are uninformative, and people who trust scientists therefore ignore this information when forming opinions about global warming's existence. People who do not trust climate scientists, however, base their conclusions on their personal observations of nature. These low-trust individuals were especially aware of the recent decline in average world temperatures; they were the ones in our survey whose doubts about global warming have increased since 2007.

This explanation is especially significant, because it suggests that the small recent decline in the proportion of people who believe in global warming is likely to be temporary. IF THE EARTH'S TEMPERATURE BEGINS TO RISE AGAIN, THESE INDIVIDUALS MAY REVERSE COURSE AND REJOIN THE LARGE MAJORITY WHO STILL THINK WARMING IS REAL.

Combating Poor Relational Intelligence® about Man-Made Global Warming

Our energy policy is the overarching issue. As citizens and voters, we need to diligently work to raise our level of Relational Intelligence® when it comes to the issue of man-made global warming, and how it is being leveraged to push an energy agenda that will have our government taking control of the energy industry and establishing significant new forms of tax revenue at the expense of every taxpayer in the country. As we increase our own RQ, it is then our responsibility to begin to challenge the RQ of those around us regarding man-made global warming – especially our elected officials.

To find out who your elected officials are and how to contact them – both at state and federal levels – online go to:

http://www.usa.gov/Contact/Elected.shtml

OR CALL THEM AT:

1 (800) FED INFO—THAT'S 1-800-333-4636

When you access the website and/or call USA.gov, you will be able to get contact and other information about the elected officials at both federal and state levels who represent you in government. You will be able to send your questions, comments and concerns to the President or his staff. You can search for your senators by name, state or congressional class and visit their websites. You can find contact information for your U.S. representative by typing in your ZIP code. By selecting your state, you will be able to access the telephone number and postal contact information for your governor. You can get the names of your state legislators and other elected officials by entering your ZIP code.

Armed with this information, you can then contact **YOUR** elected representatives and:

- ○ Demand that they call for congressional investigations about the real science behind man-made carbon dioxide.
- ○ Demand that government officials explain why they continue to support expensive and useless ethanol policies.
- ○ Demand to know why Congress isn't investigating itself for the thousands of deaths their CAFE standards have caused.
- ○ Demand to know why Congress isn't pursuing nuclear power as an alternative to foreign oil.

Even more importantly, remind your elected officials that while so much time and attention is being spent addressing all of the man-made global warming hysteria, there are many issues that are being ignored – serious problems like secure energy supplies, protection of our environment from surface pollution (something we can actually make some positive changes in) and shortfalls in education, social security, Medicare and Medicaid, etc. Life is about making decisions and decisions are about trade-offs. Tell Congress that you want them to make more relationally intelligent decisions which addresses real problems and scientific research that will let us cope with these real problems more efficiently. Or, you can allow our government to remain relationally ignorant and act on unreasonable fears that suppress energy use, economic growth and the benefits that come from the creation of national wealth.

Don't allow your single voice to be the only one that is questioning government positions and policies on man-made global warming. Educate your families and friends, as well, so that more and more people can fight back against the man-made global warming hoax.

APPENDIX A OF THIS BOOK PROVIDES BRIEF SUMMARIES OF THE KEY IDEAS PRESENTED IN THIS BOOK IN THE FORM OF FREQUENTLY ASKED QUESTIONS AND THEIR ANSWERS. They are meant to offer you a quick reference guide when you begin to engage others regarding their Relational Intelligence® about man-made global warming. These summaries succinctly capture the major arguments of the topics in this book allowing you to be able to quickly share with others the truth about the man-made global warming hoax. Go out and educate, influence and leverage your heightened Relational Intelligence® to others – be they neighbors, friends, family members or others in your community. Get them to contact their elected officials as well. It is only if we raise the collective RQ regarding man-made global warming across the country, and across the globe, that we will be able to stem the flow of misinformation that is permitting our government to institute further man-made global warming policies that will cost us more than we can ever imagine – politically, economically, socially and personally.

APPENDIX A

**FREQUENTLY ASKED QUESTIONS ABOUT
MAN-MADE GLOBAL WARMING AND THEIR ANSWERS**

In this book, we have covered many different topics related to the man-made global warming hoax. The next few pages are dedicated to summarizing the findings in an easy to follow question and answer format in order to provide a ready reference to draw upon as you continue to expand your own Relational Intelligence® regarding man-made global warming, as well as begin to question others around you about their RQ on the subject.

GREENHOUSE GASES, CARBON DIOXIDE & GLOBAL TEMPERATURE

Q| IS IT TRUE THAT CO_2 IS THE MOST PREVALENT OF ALL GREENHOUSE GASES AND THAT MAN IS THE MAJOR CONTRIBUTOR TO THESE GASES?

A| NO! AND NO!

MAN PRODUCED CO_2 CONTRIBUTES LESS THAN ONE TENTH OF ONE PERCENT TO ALL GREENHOUSE GASES. CO_2 IS ACTUALLY A BENEFICIAL AND LIFE GIVING GAS.

Greenhouse gases are at the heart of the man-made global warming argument. Of these gases, the major culprit identified by man-made global warming aficionados is carbon dioxide (CO_2). Specifically, CO_2 produced by man! In the data and charts showcased for the cause, CO_2 is always depicted as being **THE** greenhouse gas showing that total CO_2 makes up over 99 percent of all greenhouse gases. But, these charts fail to include one very important greenhouse gas – one that undermines all of the man-made global warming arguments. The gas – WATER VAPOR – which actually makes up 95 percent of all greenhouse gases (see charts on the next page).

When water vapor is rightfully included in the mix, CO_2 takes its proper place in the greenhouse gas line up contributing only a minor **3.62** PERCENT to the total greenhouse gas mix. How much of that 3.62 percent is emitted by man? Only 8 gigatons of CO_2 is emitted by man annually. Compared to the 40,000 gigatons emitted each year by our oceans, a relationally intelligent person can easily see that man's contribution to CO_2 is miniscule having virtually little or no effect on the environment at all. ACTUALLY, MAN-PRODUCED CO_2 REPRESENTS ONLY **0.117** PERCENT OF ALL GREENHOUSE GASES

Even still, what so many man-made global warming fanatics fail to realize is that carbon dioxide is a naturally occurring and life-giving gas. It is not the planet killer the man-made global warming cause would have you believe. Increased CO_2 levels promote tree and plant grown. Thanks to slightly elevated CO_2 levels, TREES ARE GROWING FASTER IN THE U.S., AND THE AMAZON RAIN FORESTS ARE GAINING TWO TONS OF BIOMASS PER ACRE PER YEAR. The crux of the matter is that while man-made CO_2 and global temperatures have been rising slightly at the same time, this does not mean that one causes the other. What we have is a COINCIDENTAL CORRELATION, one which the relationally intelligent should be able to identify and properly assess when it comes to the hoax that is man-made global warming.

Greenhouse Gas Concentrations – The Falsehood
Natural and Man-Made Sources Combined

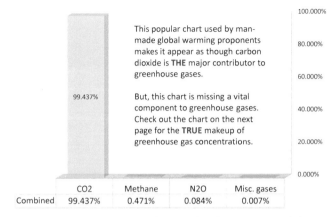

This popular chart used by man-made global warming proponents makes it appear as though carbon dioxide is **THE** major contributor to greenhouse gases.

But, this chart is missing a vital component to greenhouse gases. Check out the chart on the next page for the **TRUE** makeup of greenhouse gas concentrations.

	CO2	Methane	N2O	Misc. gases
Combined	99.437%	0.471%	0.084%	0.007%

Source: "Water Vapor Rules the Greenhouse System." From the website, Global Warming: A closer look at the numbers. Available at http://www.geocraft.com/WVFossils/greenhouse_data.html

Greenhouse Gas Concentrations – The TRUTH
Natural and Man-Made Sources

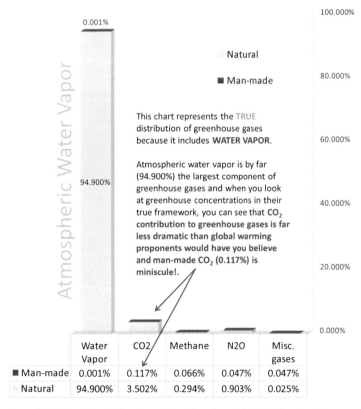

This chart represents the TRUE distribution of greenhouse gases because it includes **WATER VAPOR**.

Atmospheric water vapor is by far (94.900%) the largest component of greenhouse gases and when you look at greenhouse concentrations in their true framework, you can see that CO_2 contribution to greenhouse gases is far less dramatic than global warming proponents would have you believe and man-made CO_2 (0.117%) is miniscule!.

	Water Vapor	CO2	Methane	N2O	Misc. gases
■ Man-made	0.001%	0.117%	0.066%	0.047%	0.047%
Natural	94.900%	3.502%	0.294%	0.903%	0.025%

Source: "Water Vapor Rules the Greenhouse System." From the website, Global Warming: A closer look at the numbers. Available at http://www.geocraft.com/WVFossils/greenhouse_data.html

THE OVERALL BIG PICTURE
Greenhouse Gas Concentrations
And the Truth about Man-Made CO_2

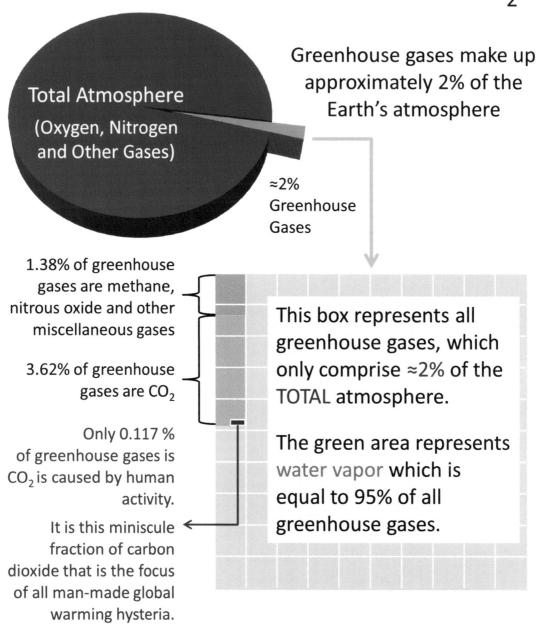

Greenhouse gases make up approximately 2% of the Earth's atmosphere

Total Atmosphere
(Oxygen, Nitrogen and Other Gases)

≈2% Greenhouse Gases

1.38% of greenhouse gases are methane, nitrous oxide and other miscellaneous gases

3.62% of greenhouse gases are CO_2

Only 0.117 % of greenhouse gases is CO_2 is caused by human activity.

It is this miniscule fraction of carbon dioxide that is the focus of all man-made global warming hysteria.

This box represents all greenhouse gases, which only comprise ≈2% of the TOTAL atmosphere.

The green area represents water vapor which is equal to 95% of all greenhouse gases.

Source: "A Global Warming Primer," National Center for Policy Analysis, 2007.
Available at http://www.ncpa.org/pdfs/GlobalWarmingPrimer.pdf

GLOBAL TEMPERATURES

Q| HOW MUCH OF A TEMPERATURE INCREASE ARE PEOPLE WORRIED ABOUT WHEN IT COMES TO MAN-MADE GLOBAL WARMING?

A| THE ANSWER IS **1.2** DEGREES CELSIUS!
THAT IS IT! BARELY OVER ONE DEGREE IS WHAT ALL THE FUSS IS ABOUT.

To put this answer into perspective, the Earth's temperature for the last 3,000 years has vacillated between +/- 3 degrees Celsius. The warming that everyone is in an uproar about is actually completely within the global norms for our planet. More importantly, the current warming trend we have been experiencing over the last 150 years is indicative of our recovery from a time known as the Little Ice Age (1250-1650). During the Little Ice Age, average global temperatures were a little over one degree cooler than they are now. Going back a bit further in time, we come to another period known as the Medieval Warm Period or Medieval Climate Optimum (800-1300). During this time, average global temperatures were over one degree warmer than they are now! Unlike what man-made global warming enthusiasts would have us believe (i.e., the world would be thrown in chaos as a result of this increase in temperatures), the Medieval Warm Period was a time of bountiful harvests and great economic prosperity, especially for European nations.

Both the Little Ice Age and the Medieval Warming Period came about before man ever started burning oil for fuel and emitting any type of carbon dioxide other than by just breathing. The **REAL** reason global temperatures fluctuate has nothing at all to do with man and everything to do with the **SUN**. SOLAR ACTIVITY IS THE ONLY SCIENTIFICALLY VALID CAUSE OF TEMPERATURE FLUCTUATIONS ON OUR PLANET. The reason for the recent overall rise in global temperatures (despite the fact that we have been in a slight cooling trend since 1998) is that solar activity has also been on the rise. The fact that this rise in temperatures coincides with man's use of hydrocarbon fuels is only that – coincidental. To state otherwise is proof of a further lack of Relational Intelligence®. Only the sun is powerful enough to affect our climate.

WHY THE MYTH OF MAN-MADE GLOBAL WARMING PERSISTS

Q | HOW DID THE MYTH OF MAN-MADE GLOBAL WARMING GET STARTED IN THE FIRST PLACE AND WHY HAS IT PERSISTED FOR SO LONG?

A | FAULTY SCIENCE LED TO THE INITIAL IDEA THAT MAN'S USE OF HYDROCARBON FUELS COULD LEAD TO A RISE IN GLOBAL TEMPERATURE. THE IDEA HAS PERSISTED DUE TO A COMBINATION OF POLITICAL MACHINATION, SCIENTIFIC TRIBALISM, MEDIA MANIPULATION AND A LACK OF RELATIONAL INTELLIGENCE® IN GOVERNMENT AND BY THE PUBLIC.

Going back as early as 1827, Josephe Fourier is the first to be credited with the idea that the Earth's atmosphere traps heat radiated by the sun. One of many gases responsible for warming the Earth is carbon dioxide (CO_2), which is both naturally occurring in the environment, but also a byproduct of the burning of hydrocarbon fuels such as oil. In the 1930's, Guy Challender was the first to suggest that man's use of hydrocarbon fuels could have an impact on global temperatures. Guy Challender could not have had it more wrong, but the man-made global warming train had already left the station. Despite an Ice Age scare in the 1970's and the fact that we have been in a slight cooling period for the past 12 years, the man-made global warming myth continues to persist for several reasons.

One of these reasons is the ENORMOUS POLITICAL ADVANTAGE gained through the continued perpetuation of man-made global warming. In these times when our nation's political and economic stability is so intertwined with other nations around the globe, it is difficult to find a "common enemy" with which to galvanize the public. But, man-made global warming is a cause that politicians can easily and effectively leverage to gain public attention and support. It has become a global "rallying cry" and, as such, is leveraged coveted by public officials (and the media). Man-made global warming is one of the few issues today that can secure immediate attention and support from the American public to push numerous agendas, regardless of their consequences. Many in our government are doing everything in their power to keep their man-made global warming on the front burner, even including the covering up of the real scientific truth about their beloved cause.

This leads to the second reason behind the perpetuation of the man-made global warming hoax: SCIENTIFIC CREDIBILITY THROUGH SCIENTIFIC TRIBALISM. Despite the flood of new data refuting that man has any significant impact on the Earth's climate, a huge number of scientists continue to staunchly defend their now defrauded data. Why? Their credibility and their grant monies (funded by our government) are at stake. In order to defend their dying cause, these pseudo-scientists pool together at various institutions to continue pushing man-made global warming agenda, even if it means falsifying their own data. The "Climategate" revelation in 2009, in which a host of emails were made public proving that man-made global warming scientists collude to hide the truth that man has absolutely no impact on global temperatures, was a first real death knoll to scientific tribalism supporting global warming. Now, more and more scientists are coming out against man-made global warming, and unlike their colleagues in the past who were ridiculed and censured for speaking against the "accepted" agenda, are actually finding a more receptive audience for their message. But, their voices are still being drowned out by the popular media's love of a good catastrophe story.

It is the media's deliberate and strategic manipulation of the public's "CATASTROPHIC MINDSET" that is the third reason the man-made global warming hoax persists today. Hominid brains are wired to always be on the lookout for threats to our survival. Our brains are still wired with the same survival triggers as our early ancestors who both hunted and were hunted back in the Pleistocene Era. So, when we hear that the world is going to become so warm that our own existence is threatened, we are on the hook. Once they tap into our "catastrophic mindset," we will listen and buy into whatever the media sells us, even if the "facts" they provide us are completely untrue. For the media, man-made global warming is good business and it is their best interest to keep believing the hype versus sharing the real truth.

The final and most troubling reason the man-made global warming hoax persists is that PEOPLE LACK THE RELATIONAL INTELLIGENCE® TO SEE THIS ISSUE FOR WHAT IT IS: A HIGHLY PROFITABLE POLITICAL PLOY TO GAIN PUBLIC SUPPORT FOR SEVERAL VERY HIGHLY SUSPECT PIECES OF LEGISLATION. Not only will this legislation potentially cost American taxpayers trillions of dollars and threaten our economy as a whole, but it will effectively hand over control of the energy industry to the government.

Q| WITH ALL OF THE CONTRARY DATA AGAINST MAN-MADE GLOBAL WARMING WHY DO SO MANY PEOPLE CONTINUE TO BELIEVE IN MAN-MADE GLOBAL WARMING?

A| A MAJOR REASON HAS TO WITH AN ASTOUNDING LACK OF SOMETHING CALLED RELATIONAL INTELLIGENCE®.

The full definition of Relational Intelligence® is:

> **RELATIONAL INTELLIGENCE®** IS THE ABILITY TO PERCEIVE AND MENTALLY PROCESS DATA, INFORMATION, ASSESS RISK AND PERCEIVE CAUSE AND EFFECT IN WAYS THAT ENABLE YOU TO LEARN, GAIN INSIGHT AND CAPITALIZE ON THE DYNAMICS OF RELATIONSHIPS AT BOTH **MICRO** AND **MACRO** LEVELS.

A key function of Relational Intelligence® is the ability to see how ideas and beliefs relate to one another and are affected by emotion/feeling versus reason. It is most people's poor Relational Intelligence® that allows them to continue to believe in man-made global warming. The human brain is wired to edit in, edit out and rearrange information to meet existing and recognizable patterns already established in the mind. As such, people exhibit COGNITIVE CONSISTENCY SYNDROME, whereby they readily accept information that confirms/conforms to their current beliefs, and systematically ignore or distort information that is contrary to these beliefs. In other words, once people make up their minds about a concept or idea (like man-made global warming), they subconsciously look for data that supports their view and systematically screen out contrary information.

So, even when faced with irrefutable data that man does not and cannot affect global temperatures, people do not have the Relational Intelligence® to overcome their belief that man-made global warming not only exists, but is such a threat to our existence that it warrants numerous ill-advised government policies and agendas.

Stronger Hurricanes and Tornados

Q| WHAT ABOUT ALL OF THE PREDICTIONS THAT MAN-MADE GLOBAL WARMING IS CAUSING MORE NUMEROUS AND MORE DANGEROUS HURRICANES AND TORNADOS?

A| THERE IS NO EVIDENCE THAT THIS IS THE CASE! HURRICANES AND TORNADOS ARE NOT ANY MORE NUMEROUS OR POWERFUL THAN THEY HAVE BEEN BEFORE MAN STARTING MAKING USE OF HYDROCARBON FUELS.

Despite all of the media hype to the contrary, there is no evidence that hurricanes and tornados are gaining in strength or in number. There has been no increase in the number of hurricanes for the last 100 years, and there has been no increase in maximum wind speed for that last 60 years.

As for tornados, the number of severe tornados in the United States has been decreasing since 1950. In fact, since 1950, WORLD HYDROCARBON USE HAS INCREASED SIX-FOLD WHILE VIOLENT TORNADO ACTIVITY FREQUENCY DECREASED BY **43** PERCENT!

The reason for all the recent concern over these powerful storms stems not from changes in the storms themselves, but from the fact that we have moved ourselves and our property into areas not safe from these storms. As people continue to build more and more expensive homes on beach front property and, as in the case of New Orleans, cities spread into former marsh lands, when a storm comes, the damage toll is much higher. Again, the storms themselves are not stronger... people just have more to lose.

Q&A SIX |

LACK OF THREAT TO POLAR BEARS AND PENGUINS

Q| WHAT ABOUT ALL THE TALK ABOUT MAN-MADE GLOBAL WARMING KILLING OFF ALL OF THE POLAR BEARS AND PENGUINS?

A| NONE OF IT IS TRUE! POLAR BEAR AND PENGUIN POPULATIONS ARE ACTUALLY DOING JUST FINE IN SLIGHTLY WARMER TEMPERATURES.

The canaries of the man-made global warming movement – polar bears and penguins – are actually flourishing. Despite misleading photographs and false information present by man-made global warming devotees, polar bear populations are higher now than any time in the 20th century. IN 1960, THERE WERE ONLY 5,000 BEARS. TODAY, THERE ARE OVER 25,000. Even more damning for global warming cultists is that the territories where polar bear subpopulations are in decline have actually been getting colder over the past 50 years. THE AREAS WHERE POLAR BEARS ARE STABLE AND/OR FLOURISHING ARE GETTING WARMER!

As for penguins, their population numbers are also on the rise. Empire penguins (the ones from the movie, **March of the Penguins**) are not endangered as many people believe. They are in the category of "least concern" by the International Union for Conservation of Natural and Natural Resource. Penguin populations in Antarctica and elsewhere have been stable or increasing for the last 30 years, despite the docudramas suggesting the contrary.

The Polar Bear Population Growth

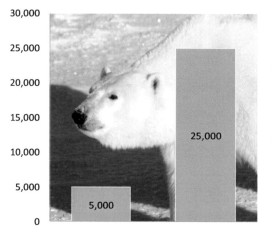

Polar bear numbers increased dramatically from around 5,000 in the 1960s to as many as 25,000 today, higher than at any time in the 20th century.

Of the distinct polar bear populations worldwide, only two populations are decreasing. The majority of the populations are stable or increasing.

Source: Stefan Norris, Lynn Rosentrater and Pal Martin Eid, "Polar Bears at Risk: A WWF Status Report, "World Wildlife Fund, May 2002.
Available at http://www.wwf.org.uk/filelibrary/pdf/polar_bears_at_risk_report.pdf

CONSENSUS SCIENCE ABOUT MAN-MADE GLOBAL WARMING

Q| AL GORE AND OTHERS ASSERT THAT THERE IS A "CONSENSUS" AMONG SCIENTISTS ABOUT MAN-MADE GLOBAL WARMING. IS THIS TRUE?

A| ABSOLUTELY NOT! NOTHING COULD BE FURTHER FROM THE TRUTH. MORE AND MORE SCIENTISTS ARE COMING OUT AGAINST "DATA" THAT SUPPORTS MAN-MADE GLOBAL WARMING.

President Barack Obama, former Vice President Al Gore, and many others have been repeatedly quoted saying that the "science" of man-made global warming is irrefutable. This is completely untrue! An ever growing number within the scientific community are coming out against the false data behind man-made global warming… and they are coming out against those "scientists" who promote this false data.

One hot button of contention is the infamous "hockey stick" global temperature chart originally presented by Michael Mann. Mann's "hockey stick" chart showed a dramatic increase in global temperatures over the last 100 years compared to the last 1,000 years. The Intergovernmental Panel on Climate Change (IPCC) immediately adopted Mann's chart as key evidence of man-made global warming. However, it soon came to light that Mann had deliberately ignored data showing the Little Ice Age and the Medieval Warming Period. These two periods of global temperature fluctuation were simply eliminated from Mann's data, thereby allowing the recent warming trends to take on considerably more significance. THIS BLATANT MANIPULATION OF DATA RESULTED IN AN OUTCRY IN THE SCIENTIFIC COMMUNITY. The Little Ice Age and the Medieval Warming Period were accepted phenomenon having been tested and retested in several different studies. The fact that Mann simply disregarded this data without any explanation stepped far beyond the accepted bounds of many of Mann's fellow climatologists. When asked for copies of his original data, Mann was either unwilling or unable to share with his colleagues. Mann's chart became such a contested issue that the IPCC was forced to drop it from its man-made global warming arsenal of "evidence." Ultimately, Mann still stands behind his chart, but a congressional investigation of his findings left most other scientists rejecting Mann's data for what it was – total misinformation.

Additional proof of how man-made global warming scientists are willing to "sacrifice" their morality to perpetuate their cause came when a number of emails became public featuring discussions between scientists about whether certain scientific data should be released if it did not directly support man-made global warming. "CLIMATEGATE," as it was named, brought into high relief how readily scientists were willing to hide the truth about man-made global warming. One of the most damning statements that came out of Climategate emails was the phrase, "we must hide the decline," referring to the actual slight DECREASE in global temperatures since 1998. Any evidence to the contrary is simply swept under the rug so the hoax could live on.

And CLIMATEGATE was not an isolated incident. More and more stories are coming to light where data has been manipulated, hidden or destroyed that might contradict man-made global warming. From the EPA to NASA, from academia to Wikipedia, there continues to be a full-on push to hide the truth that man in no way affects global temperatures. But, the tide has turned. Too many reputable scientists are coming out against the "data" behind man-made global warming to be ignored. INDEED, THE GLOBAL WARMING PETITION PROJECT THAT - *26.STARTED IN 1998 NOW HAS OVER 17,100 SIGNATURES FROM AMERICAN SCIENTISTS (INCLUDING OVER 9,000 PH.D.'S).

ETHANOL & THE MAN-MADE GLOBAL WARMING HOAX

Q| IS ETHANOL A BETTER FUEL THAN GASOLINE?

A| NO! ETHANOL IS A NON-SUSTAINABLE FUEL ALTERNATIVE/ADDITIVE THAT IS NOT ONLY COSTLY BUT MORE ENVIRONMENTALLY DAMAGING THAN GASOLINE.

Back in 2006, the government mandated a five-fold increase in the production of ethanol in order to reduce our dependence on foreign oil, to have a greener, more environmentally-friendly fuel, and to provide support for farmers in the heart-land of our country. However, ethanol has not only failed to live up to these expectations, but has also resulted in several unintended consequences.

Our dependence on foreign oil will remain despite the government's push for ethanol, especially corn-based ethanol. Even if we dedicated all of the land from our corn and soybean crops each year to the production of ethanol, it would only displace 18 percent of our national gasoline consumption. When you factor in how much energy would be required to produce this ethanol, GASOLINE DEMAND WOULD ONLY BE REDUCED BY 5 PERCENT. Crop area restraints, resource limitations and high energy input required to produce ethanol negate any hope that ethanol could reduce our dependence on foreign oil. In addition, the cost of producing ethanol will most likely decrease our use of U.S. domestic oil because foreign oil is still significantly cheaper to refine than the oil we produce in this country. As ethanol fills more of our tanks, we will keep using foreign oil because it is simply too cheap to pass up.

Ethanol production has already caused a serious increase in the price of corn. REMEMBER, BETWEEN 2007 AND APRIL 2008, THE PRICE OF CORN ROSE 66 PERCENT. The resulting rise in all food costs will continue to have a significant impact on our nation's poor and the hungry of the world. Already 17 million American families have trouble putting food on their tables. How many more will go hungry as the government takes more and more corn out of our mouths and turns it into ethanol?

Rather than providing new life for our country's small farmers, the government's push for ethanol has provided fantastic new revenue for the largest agribusiness conglomerates like Archer Daniels Midland and Cargill. These companies want to keep their lion's share of the estimated 6.3 billion dollars to 8.7 billion dollars of ethanol subsidy monies paid by federal and state governments each year. As a result, the push for ethanol has created a powerful agriculture industry lobby that is writing big checks to our presidential, congressional and state official candidates to ensure that ethanol remains a government priority, regardless of the issues surrounding its production and use.

Finally, corn-based ethanol is anything but "green." ONE GALLON OF ETHANOL PRODUCES ONLY 67 PERCENT OF THE ENERGY FOUND IN A GALLON OF GASOLINE AND, DEPENDING ON THE TYPE OF ETHANOL FUEL BLEND, GETS ANYWHERE BETWEEN 4 PERCENT AND 25 PERCENT FEWER MILES TO THE GALLON. Ethanol refineries are heavy polluters and have been fined by the Environmental Protection Agency (EPA) on numerous occasions for exceeding maximum emissions standards. Once ethanol is in our fuel tanks, it continues to pollute, releasing several toxic emissions into the air that cause a variety of health and environmental issues. Furthermore, corn is a nutrient-intensive crop characterized by heavy soil tillage, fertilizer and pesticide use. The production of additional corn for ethanol will only exacerbate the environmental effects of soil erosion and water pollution, including almost certainly increasing the size of the Gulf of Mexico Dead Zone. The runoff of excess nitrogen and phosphorus from agricultural fertilizers is promoting an excess amount of algae, which depletes the water of essential oxygen, killing off huge numbers of fish and other marine life. AS A RESULT, THE SEAFOOD INDUSTRY HAS BEEN HARD HIT GIVEN THAT 72 PERCENT OF HARVEST SHRIMP, 66 PERCENT OF HARVEST OYSTERS AND 16 PERCENT OF COMMERCIAL FISH COME FROM THE GULF OF MEXICO.

CAFE Standards

Q | WHAT DO CAFE STANDARDS HAVE TO DO WITH MAN-MADE GLOBAL WARMING, AND ARE THEY INDICATIVE OF GOVERNMENT POLICIES THAT RESULT IN UNEXPECTED AND DANGEROUS CONSEQUENCES?

A | CAFE STANDARDS WERE INSTITUTED BY THE GOVERNMENT TO REDUCE FUEL CONSUMPTION OF AMERICAN DRIVERS. RATHER THAN SAVING ON GASOLINE, CAFE STANDARDS HAVE MADE CARS MORE DANGEROUS... EVEN DEADLY.

Corporate Average Fuel Economy (CAFE) standards in this country are forcing automakers to build lighter and more dangerous vehicles. In order to meet the miles per gallon restrictions of 35 mpg set by the Energy Policy Conservation Act, automakers will make lighter cars the norm. At the moment, less than a dozen out of 1,100 vehicles meet the standard. As such, we can expect all cars to become lighter and thus, more lethal. There is a 1.1 percent increase in fatalities per 100 lbs. of vehicle weight. A study by NATIONAL HIGHWAY TRAFFIC SAFETY ADMINISTRATION concluded that the downsizing resulted in UP TO 2,000 ADDITIONAL DEATHS AND 20,000 ADDITIONAL SERIOUS OR MODERATE INJURIES PER YEAR! American lives are coming under more and more risk simply to try and offset a ridiculous 0.117 percent of man-made carbon dioxide that people falsely believe is causing climate change.

MAN-MADE GLOBAL WARMING AND CAP & TRADE

Q| THE GOVERNMENT IS PROPOSING CARBON CAP & TRADE LEGISLATION UNDER THE GUISE OF RESPONDING THE MAN-MADE GLOBAL WARMING ISSUE. WHAT IS CARBON CAP & TRADE, AND WHAT CONSEQUENCES WILL IT HAVE ON THE ENERGY INDUSTRY, OUR ECONOMY AND OUR LIVES?

A| THE CARBON CAP & TRADE PROGRAM WILL BASICALLY ALLOW THE GOVERNMENT TO GAIN CONTROL OVER THE ENERGY INDUSTRY AND MAKE ENERGY SO COSTLY FOR INDIVIDUALS AND FAMILIES AS TO THROW OUR ECONOMY INTO CHAOS.

The carbon cap & trade program is potentially the most dangerous of all the programs being pursued as a result of the man-made global warming hoax. The consequences of cap & trade will reach far beyond any other piece of legislation currently on the books to combat climate change. In essence, our government intends to create a massive carbon commodities market under the guise of reducing carbon emissions. By establishing and distributing carbon emission credits that companies can buy and sell to meet new and more restrictive carbon emission standards, the government is in effect creating an energy tax – one that will impact every American and global citizen. It is estimated that in 10 years, cap & trade will increase energy costs by an additional 1,288 dollars per household. By 2035, that cost would soar to 6,800 dollars per household. Bearing the brunt of these costs are lower income families who will find that approximately 40 percent of their total income will have to be dedicated to energy costs alone.

But, whereas the American family will suffer, big corporations and our government will reap huge profits as a result of cap & trade. It is estimated that cap & trade would become a 10 trillion dollar commodities market. Compare this to the fact that the New York Stock Exchange is currently worth between 19 and 21 trillion dollars; you get some idea of the huge impact Cap & Trade could have on our economy. And, if cap & trade somehow fails to become law (it has passed in the House already), the government has a back-up plan using the Environmental Protection Agency. The EPA is already putting stronger restrictions on carbon emissions. One way or another, the government is fixed on its course to limit carbon emissions, regardless of the impact on the economic stability of the nation.

NUCLEAR POWER

Q| NEEDLESS MAN-MADE GLOBAL WARMING FEARS ASIDE, THERE IS A REAL NEED TO REDUCE OUR RELIANCE ON FOREIGN OIL AS OUR MAJOR ENERGY SOURCE. ARE THERE ANY ALTERNATIVE FUEL SOURCES THAT COULD MEET OUR FUTURE ENERGY DEMANDS QUICKLY AND RELIABLY?

A| YES! NUCLEAR FUEL NOT ONLY REDUCES CARBON EMISSIONS, BUT IS A TECHNOLOGY WE CAN LEVERAGE ALMOST IMMEDIATELY TO REDUCE OUR RELIANCE ON FOREIGN ENERGY. IN ADDITION, NUCLEAR FUEL HAS THE POTENTIAL TO BECOME A HUGE FINANCIAL BOON FOR OUR COUNTRY.

There is a REAL alternative energy source that could actually benefit our country: nuclear power. While man-made global warming is a hoax, there are other reasons why as a country we must find alternative fuel sources. Currently, we are net importer of energy. We are reliant on foreign oil to keep our country running. However, if we truly harnessed the potential of nuclear power, the United States could become a net exporter of energy, not only become energy independent, but create a new and profitable form of trade that would benefit our economy (not harm it as in the case of cap & trade). Nuclear energy is emission-free, cost-effective and the quickest strategy to move us out of our current state of energy dependence. However, before we can tap into the potential that is nuclear power, we once again must face the lack of Relational Intelligence® by much of the public and by our government. Regulations have made building nuclear power facilities so cumbersome that energy companies are completely hamstrung in their attempts to expand our use of nuclear power. Once again, the government is showing its agenda in controlling the energy industry and claiming it as its own.

THE TRUTH ABOUT AL GORE & MAN-MADE GLOBAL WARMING

Q| DOES AL GORE REALLY HAVE OUR COUNTRY'S BEST INTEREST AT HEART AS HE CHAMPIONS THE MAN-MADE GLOBAL WARMING CAUSE?

A| NO! AL GORE IS SETTING HIMSELF UP TO BE THE FIRST CLIMATE BILLIONAIRE!

Al Gore's efforts on behalf of "his" cause are anything but selfless and altruistic. Rather, Al Gore is a modern day sophist using rhetoric and outright falsehoods to further a belief that he not only does not live by, but uses to line his own pockets. AL GORE STANDS TO BENEFIT GREATLY FROM PROPOSED "CAP-AND-TRADE" AND OTHER LEGISLATION — AND POSSIBLY BECOME THE FIRST "CLIMATE BILLIONAIRE." He has made millions of dollars in private energy ventures first in his role as partner in Kleiner, Perkins, Caufield & Byers, a venture capital firm that invests in technology to address global warming. Also, through his London-based startup company called Generation Investment Management (GIM), founded with three former bigwigs from Goldman Sachs Asset Management, David Blood, Mark Ferguson and Peter Harris, Gore stands to reap huge profits from cap-and-trade legislation that would mandate carbon trading.

As for Gore's Goldman Sachs partners, they also have their hands in the carbon allowance cookie jar. Goldman Sachs holds 11.75 percent interest in Climate Exchange PLC, which, in turn owns the Chicago Climate Exchange – the exchange where corporations will buy, sell, and trade the government's carbon credits. Like all commodity exchanges, the Chicago Climate Exchange charges a commission on all trades made on the exchange. IF THE CAP-AND-TRADE BILL PASSES, CARBON TRADERS AND GOLDMAN SACHS WILL MAKE MILLIONS, POSSIBLY BILLIONS, FROM COMMISSIONS ON CARBON TRADING.

Even without Al Gore's intent to receive personal gain through his own cause, his massive carbon footprint from his home in Tennessee (which consumes 20 times more energy than the national average) and his many other properties, Gore shows his true motto for man-made global warming – do as I say and not as I do. From Al's own massive carbon footprint to how he and his pals are set to make billions off trading CO_2, Al Gore is "Exhibit A" for how a lack of Relational Intelligence® on the part of the American public is allowing the government to institute policies that will have a devastating impact both on our national economy, and on our own personal pocketbooks.

ENDNOTES

The author is indebted to Dr. Martin Stickley for his suggestions on the science included in this book. The author also acknowledges two specific presentations he relied on from Dr. Stickley:

- C. Martin Stickley. "Background on Global Warming." July 28, 2008 and "Alternative Views about Global Warming." Feb 25, 2009. Presented to the US Chamber of Commerce, Washington, DC

chapter one | THE MAN-MADE GLOBAL WARMING ISSUE

1. Levitt, Steven D. and Stephen J. Dubner. *Super Freakonomics: Global Cooling, Patriotic Prostitutes and Why Suicide Bombers Should Buy Life Insurance.* New York: HarperCollins Publishers. 2009. Print.

2. Lindzen, Richard S. "Global Warming: The Origin and Nature of the Alleged Scientific Consensus." Cato Review of Business & Government. 1992. Available at: http://www.cato.org/pubs/regulation/regv15n2/v15n2-9.pdf

3. Lizeberman, Ben. "Frequently Asked Questions About Global Warming." The Heritage Foundation. 21 March 2007. Available at: http://www.heritage.org/Research/EnergyandEnvironment/wm1403.cfm

4. Lomborg, Bjorn. *Cool It: The Skeptical Environmentalist's Guide to Global Warming.* New York: Alfred. A. Knopf. 2007. Print.

5. Williams, Walter. "We've Been Had!" *Whistleblower* Feb 2010: 12-21. Print.

chapter two | THE LACK OF RELATIONAL INTELLIGENCE® REGARDING MAN-MADE GLOBAL WARMING

1. "Correlation does not imply causation." *Wikipedia.org.* 1 April 2010. Available at: http://en.wikipedia.org/wiki/correlation_does_not_imply_causation

2. Huseman, Richard C. *Leader as Coach.* Equity Press. 2008. Print.

3. Huseman, Richard C. *How the Brain Works.* Equity Press. 2009. Print.

4. Huseman, Richard C. "Relational Intelligence®." *Coaching Update.* n.d. Print.

5. Levitt, Steven D. and Stephen J. Dubner. *Freakonomics.* New York: HarperCollins Publishers. 2009. Print.

6. "Radon Causes 100 Times More Deaths than Carbon Monoxide Poisoning." *Right Truth.* 2 Jan 2009. Available at: http://righttruth.typepad.com/right_truth/2009/01/radon-causes-100-times-more-deaths-than-carbon-monoxide-poisoning.html

7. Shuttleworth, Martyn. "Correlation and Causation." *Experiment-resources.com.* 2008. Available at: http://www.experiment-resources.com/correlation-and-causation.html

chapter three | AL GORE: THE CLIMATE GOD?

1. "Al Gore's Personal Energy Use Is His Own 'Inconvenient Truth.'" Press Release. 26 February 2007. Available at: http://www.tenneseepolicy.org/main/article.php?article_id=367.

2. Baker, Brent. "Global Warming Will Cause Mass Cannibalism, Insurgents are Patriots." *NewsBusters.* 2 April 2008. Available at: http://newsbusters.org/blogs/brent-baker/2008/04/02/turner-iraqi-insurgents-patriots-inaction-warming-cannibalism

3. Beale, Lauren. "Al Gore, Tipper Gore Snap up Montecito-area Villa." *Los Angeles Times.* 28 April 2010. Available at: http://articles.latimes.com/2010/apr/28/home/la-hm-hotprop-gore-20100428

4. "Cap-and-Trade: Al Gore's Cash Cow." *Investors.com.* Investor's Business Daily. 29 April 2009. Available at: http://www.investors.com/NewsAndAnalysis/Article.aspx?id=475461

5. Gilder, Mary Ellen Tiffany. "The Gospel according to Gore." Global Warming News and Views. *SiteWave.net.* n.d. Available at: http://www.sitewave.net/news/s49p1835.htm

6. Gore, Al. "We Can't Wish Away Climate Change." *The New York Times.* 28 Feb 2010. Available at: http://www.nytimes.com/2010/02/28/opinion/28gore.html?scp=1&sq=al%20gore%20wish%20away%20climate%20change&st=cse

7. "Inconvenient truth for Al Gore as his North Pole sums don't add up." *TimesOnline.com.* 15 Dec 2009. Available at: http://www.timesonline.co.uk/tol/news/environment/copenhagen/article6956783.ece

8. "Miner's Canary." *Wikipedia.org.* 9 Feb 2010. Available at: http://en.wikipedia.org/wiki/Miner%27s_canary#Miner.27s_canary

9. "Sophists." Internet Encyclopedia of Philosophy: A Peer-Reviewed Academic Resource. 22 October 2004. Available at: http://www.iep.utm.edu/sophists

chapter four | GLOBAL TEMPERATURES: WHAT ACTUALLY CONSTITUTES WARMING?

1. Baliunas, Sallie and Willie Soon. "Climate History and the Sun." George C. Marshall Institute: Washington, D.C. 5 June 2001. Available at: http://www.marshall.org/pdf/materials/90.pdf

2. Bradley, R.S. "Climate in Medieval Time." *Science*. 302-404-405. 2003.

3. Carlisle, John. "Global Warming: Enjoy it While You Can." National Policy Analysis. No. 194. April 1998. Available at: http://www.nationalcenter.org/NPA194.html

4. Fyall, Jenny. "Warming will 'wipe out billions.'" *Scotsman.com*. Sweetness & Light. 29 Nov 2009. Available at: http://sweetness-light.com/archive/only-10-will-survive-global-warming

5. "Global Surface Temperature Anomalies." National Oceanic and Atmospheric Administration. *National Climatic Data Center*. 1 March 2010. Available at: http://www.ncdc.noaa.gov/cmb-faq/anomalies.html

6. Graybill, D.A. and Idso, S.B. "Detecting the aerial fertilization effect of atmospheric CO2 enrichment in tree ring chronologies." *Global Biogeochemical Cycle*. 7: 81-95. 1993.

7. Jacoby, Jeff. "Where's Global Warming?" *Boston.com*. The Boston Globe. 8 March 2009. Available at: http://www.boston.com/bostonglobe/editorial_opinion/oped/articles/2009/03/08/wheres_global_warming/

8. Keigwin, Lloyd D. "The Little Ice Age and Medieval Warm Period in the Sargasso Sea." Vol 274, no. 5292. Science AAAS. 29 Nov 2006. Available at: http://www.sciencemag.org/cgi/search?src=hw&site_area=sci&fulltext=Little+Ice+Age

9. Mann, M., Bradley, R.S. and Hughes, M.K. "Corrigendum: Global-scale temperature patterns and climate forcing over the past six centuries." *Nature*. 430:105. 2004.

10. Mann, M.E., Bradley R.S. and Hughes, M.K. "Global-scale temperature patterns and climate forcing over the past six centuries." *Nature*. 392:779-787. 2007.

11. McIntyre, S. and R. McKitrick. "Corrections to the Mann et al. "Proxy database and Northern Hemisphere temperature series." *Energy and Environment*. 14: 751-771. 2003.

12. Muller, Richard. "Global Warming Bombshell." *Technology Review*. MIT. 15 Oct 2007. Available at: http://www.technologyreview.com/energy/13830/

13. Rosenthal, Elisabeth. "Solar Industry Learns Lessons in Spanish Sun." *The New York Times*. 8 March 2010. Available at: http://www.nytimes.com/2010/03/09/business/energy-environment/09solar.html

14. Royer, D.L., Berner, R. A. and Park, J. "Climate sensitivity constrained by CO2 concentrations over the past 420 million years." *Nature*. 446: 530-532. 2007.

15. "Science: Another Ice Age?" *Time.com*. 24 June 1974. Available at: http://www.time.com/time/magazine/article/0,9171,944914,00.html

16. Steven, William K. "Scientist at Work: Richard S. Lindzen; A Skeptic Asks, Is It Getting Hotter, Or Is It Just the Computer Model?" *NewYorkTimes.com*. 18 June 1996. Available at: http://www.nytimes.com/1996/06/18/science/scientist-work-richard-s-lindzen-skeptic-asks-it-getting-hotter-it-just-

17. Taylor, Harry A. "Global Warming: Nature not Man." December 2009. Available at: http://www.heartland.org/custom/semod_policybot/pdf/26567.pdf

18. *US National Assessment of the Potential Consequences of Climate Variability and Change*. 2008. Available at: http://www.usgcrp.gov/usgcrp/nacc/default.htm

chapter five | GREENHOUSE GASES: IS CO$_2$ REALLY THE BAD GUY?

1. "A Global Warming Primer." National Center for Policy Analysis. 2007. Available at: http://www.ncpa.org/pdfs/GlobalWarmingPrimer.pdf

2. Abrams, Courtney "America's Biggest Polluters: Carbon Dioxide Emissions from Power Plants in 2007." Environment Oregon Research & Policy Center. Nov 2009. Available at: http://www.environmentoregon.org/uploads/3c/22/3c22bfda9778f49da4787cbd9f4c9964/Americas-Biggest-Polluters-Report-Web.pdf

3. Burnett, Sterling H. "U.S. Greenhouse Gas Emissions Decline." Global Warming Facts. *The Heartland Institute*. 30 March 2010. Available at: http://www.globalwarmingheartland.org/full/27373/US_Greenhouse_Gas_Emissions_Decline.html

4. "Carbon Dioxide Emissions From Power Plants Rated Worldwide." *ScienceDaily*. 15 Nov 2007. Available at: http://www.sciencedaily.com/releases/2007/11/071114163448.htm

5. Davidson, Vicki McClure. "Rush Limbaugh & Charlton Heston: The Vanity and Arrogance of Earth Day, Global Warming, and Climate Change." Frugal Café Blog Zone. 23 April 2009. Available at: http://www.frugal-cafe.com/public_html/frugal-blog/frugal-cafe-blogzone/2009/04/23/

6. Doyle, Alister. "Methane Bubbles in Arctic Seas Stir Global Warming Fears." Reuters News Service. *ABC News*. 4 March 2010, Available at: http://abcnews.go.com/print?id=10010948

7. Hausfather, Zeke. "The Water Vapor Feedback." 4 Feb 2008. Available at: http://www.yaleclimatemediaforum.org/2008/02/common-climate-misconceptions-the-water-vapor-feedback-2/

8. Hieb, Monte. *Global Warming: A Closer Look at the Numbers*. Geocraft. 10 Jan 2003. Available at: http://www.geocraft.com/WVFossils/greenhouse_data.html

9. "Greenhouse Gases: Frequently Asked Questions." National Oceanic and Atmospheric Administration. *National Climatic Data Center*. 20 Aug 2008. Available at: http://www.ncdc.noaa.gov/oa/climate/gases.html

10. Learn, Scott. "Report Details CO2 Emissions from Boardman, other power plants." *OregonLive.com*. Oregon Environmental News. 23 Dec 2009. Available at:http://www.oregonlive.com/environment/index.ssf/2009/12/report_details_co2_emissions_f.html

11. Mangino, Martin. "Carbon Dioxide Unlikely to Cause Higher Temperatures." *TimesDispatch.com*. Richmond Times-Dispatch. 14 March 2010. Available at:http://www2.timesdispatch.com/rtd/news/opinion/commentary/article/ED-MANG14_20100312-204009/330040/

12. Murray, Iain and H.Sterling Burnett. "10 Cool Global Warming Policies." National Center for Policy Analysis. No. 321. June 2009. Available at: http://www.ncpa.org/pdfs/st321.pdf

13. Robinson, Arthur B., Noah E. Robinson, and Willie Soon. "Environmental Effects of Increased Atmospheric Carbon Dioxide." Vol. 12. Journal of American Physicians and Surgeons. 2007. Available at: http://www.jpands.org/vol12no3/robinson.pdf

14. Rutan, Burt. "Non-Aerospace Research Quests of a Designer/Flight Test Engineer." *RPS3.com*. Version 11. 20 August 2009. Available at: http://rps3.com/Files/AGW/Rutan.AGWdataAnalysis%20v11.pdf

chapter six | **MORE INCONVENIENT TRUTHS**

1. Booker, Christopher. "Polar Bear Expert Barred by Global Warmists." *Telegraph.co.uk*. 27 June 2009. Available at: http://www.telegraph.co.uk/comment/columnists/christopherbooker/5664069/Polar-bear-expert-barred-by-global-warmists.html

2. "Effects of Climate Change on Polar Bears." *Panda.org*. WWF. n.d. Available at: http://assets.panda.org/downloads/pb_factsheet.pdf

3. Horner, Christopher C. *The Politically Incorrect Guide to Global Warming and Environmentalism*. Washington, DC: Regnery Publishing, Inc. 2007. Print.

4. Murray, Iain. *The Really Inconvenient Truths: Seven Environmental Catastrophes Liberals Don't Want You to Know About — Because They Helped Cause Them*. Washington, DC: Regnery Publishing, Inc. 2008. Print.

5. "Polar bear status, distribution & population." *WWF*. Accessed 11 Dec 2009. Available at: http://www.panda.org/what_we_do/where_we_work/arctic/area/species/polarbear/population

6. The Political Class. "Polar Bear Population on the Rise, According the Scientist, Not Declining – as the Al Gore crowd tells everyone. Polar Bear expert barred from testifying." Red State. 28 June 2009. Available at: http://www.redstate.com/kjl291/2009/06/28/polar-bear-population-on-the-rise-according-to-scientist-not-declining

chapter seven | THE UTTER LACK OF CONSENSUS SCIENCE

1. Booker, Christopher. *The Real Global Warming Disaster*. New York: Continuum International Publishing Group. 2009. Print.

2. Broder, John M. "Scientists Taking Steps to Defend Work on Climate." The New York Times. 2 March 2010. Available at: http://www.nytimes.com/2010/03/03/science/earth/03climate.html?hp=&pagewanted=print

3. "Climate Science and Candor." The Wall Street Journal. 24 Nov 2009. Available at: http://online.wsj.com/article/SB10001424052748704779704574553652849094482.html

4. "Copenhagen Consensus: The Results." Copenhagen Consensus Center. 2008. Available at: http://www.copenhagenconsensus.com

5. Derbyshire, David. "Copenhagen Climate Change Summit to Produce as much CO2 as an African Country." Mail Online. 8 Dec 2009. Available at: http://www.dailymail.co.uks/news/article-1233771.html

6. Gavin, S., J. Coon and S. P. Karrer. "The Age of the Sun: Kelvin vs. Darwin." Physics Department, Wayne State University. 2008. Available at: http://web.mac.com/kegavin/Sean/Course_information_files/kelvinsunF.pdf

7. Gilligan, Andrew. "Copenhagen Climate Summit: 1,200 limos, 140 private plans and caviar wedges." *Telegraph.co.uk*. Telegraph Media Group. 5 Dec 2009. Available at: http://www.telegraph.co.uk/earth/copenhagen-climate-change-confe/6736517/Copenhagen-climate-summit-1200-limos-140-private-planes-and-caviar-wedges.html

8. Goldberg, Jonah. "Groupthink and the Global Warming Industry." *USA Today.* 1 Dec 2009. Print.

9. "Government Monopsony Distorts Climate Science, says SPPI." *TransWorldNews.* 22 July 2009. Available at: http://www.transworldnews.com/NewsStory.aspx?id-104031&cat=12

10. Horner, Chris. "Global Warming's Missing Link: EPA Whistleblower Exposes Agenda's Fatal Flaw." Energy Tribune. 20 July 2009. Available at: http://www.energytribune.com/articles.cfm?aid=2088

11. "James Hansen's Former NASA Supervisor Declares Himself a Skeptic – Says Hansen 'Embarrassed NASA,' 'Was Never Muzzled,' & Models 'Useless'." *Watts up With That?* WordPress.com. 27 Jan 2009. Available at: http://wattsupwiththat.com/2009/01/27/james-hansens-former-nasa-supervisor-declares-himself-a-skeptic-says-hansen-embarrassed-nasa-was-never-muzzled/

12. Happer, William. Climate Science in the Political Arena. *Before the Select Committee on Energy Independence and Global Warming U.S. House of Representatives.* 20 May 2010. Available at: http://globalwarming.house.gov/files/HRG/052010SciencePolicy/happer.pdf

13. McIntyre, Steve. "Curry: On the Credibility of Climate Research." *ClimateAudit.org.* Climate Audit. 22 Nov 2009. Available at: http://climateaudit.org/2009/11/22/curry-on-the-credibility-of-climate-research/

14. McIntyre, Steve. "Gerry North Doesn't Understand the 'Trick.'" *ClimateAudit.org.* Climate Audit. 1 Dec 2009. Available at: http://camirror.wordpress.com/

15. McIntyre, Steve. "The Trick." Climate Audit. 26 Nov 2009. Available at: http://camirror.wordpress.com/2009/11/26/the-trick

16. *Montford, A.W. The Hockey Stick Illusion: Climategate and the Corruption of Science.* London: Stacey International. March 2010. Print.

17. Moskowitz, Ciara. "NASA Signs New $335 Million Deal to Fly Astronauts on Russian Spaceships." *SPACE.com.* TechMediaNetwork. 6 April 2010. Available at: http://www.space.com/news/nasa-russia-astronaut-contract-100406.htm

18. Norton-Smith, Dulcinea. "Galileo Versus Catholicism: The Teaching of the Copernican Theory that Angered the Church." *Suite101.com.* 14 March 2008. Available at: http://catholicism.suite101.com/article.cfm/galileo_versus_catholicism

19. *Petition Project.* Global Warming Petition Project. 1998-2001. Available at: http://www.oism.org/pproject/

20. Reinecker, Amanda. "What's at stake in Copenhagen?" *MyHeritage.org.* The Heritage Foundation. 8 Dec 2009. Available at: http://www.myheritage.org/archive/email/whats-at-stake-in.html

21. Skye0725 [John]. "Apparently Global Warming "Research" Needs a Federal Bailout as Well!" True Discernment. 28 Jan 2009. Available at: http://truedsicernment.com/2009/01/28/apparently-global-warming-research-needs-a-federal-bailout-as-well/

22. Revkin, Andrew C. "Hacked E-Mail Is New Fodder for Climate Dispute." *NyTimes.com*. The New York Times. 21 Nov 2009. Available at: http://www.nytimes.com/2009/11/21/science/earth/21climate.html?_r=1&scp=1&sq=Hacked%20email%20is%20new%20fodder%20for%20climate%20dispute&st=cse

23. Solomon, Lawrence. *The Deniers: The World-Renowned Scientists Who Stood Up Against Global Warming Hysteria, Political Persecution, and Fraud.* Minneapolis: Richard Vigilante Books. 2008. Print

24. Spencer, Roy W. Climate Confusion: How Global Warming Hysteria Leads to Bad Science, Pandering Politicians and Misguided Policies That Hurt the Poor. New York: Encounter Books. 2008. Print.

25. Stuart, Courteney. "Cuccinelli Targets UVA Papers in Climategate Salvo." *The Hook.* 29 April 2010. Available at: http://www.readthehook.com/blog/index.php/2010/04/29/oh-mann-cuccinelli-targets-uva-papers-in-climategate-salvo/

26. Watson, Paul Joseph. "Globalist Hypocrites Arrive in Copenhagen for Summit." *InfoWars.com.* 7 Dec 2009. Available at: http://www.infowars.com

27. Webster, Ben. "Science Chief John Beddington Calls for Honesty on Climate Change." *TimesOnline.* 27 Jan 2010. Available at: http://www.timesonline.co.uk/tol/news/environment/article7003622.ece

chapter eight | ETHANOL & THE MAN-MADE GLOBAL WARMING HOAX

1. "An Earful on Ethanol: Rising Food Prices, Inefficient Production and Other Problems." *Knowledge@Wharton*. 28 May 2008. Available at: http://knowledge.wharton.upenn.edu/article.cfm?articleid=1972

2. "Biorefinery Locations." Renewable Fuels Association. n.d. Available at: http://www.ethanolrfa.org/industry/locations

3. Brown, Lester R. "Insights: Why Ethanol Production Will Drive World Food Prices Even Higher in 2008." Environment News Services. 25 Jan. 2008. Available at: http://www.ens-newswire.com/ens/jan2008/2008-01-25-insbro.asp

4. Choi, Charles Q. "Surprise: Ethanol as Deadly as Gasoline for Now." *Live Science*. TechMediaNetwork.com. 18 April 2007. Available at: http://auto.howstuffworks.com/fuel-efficiency/alternative-fuels/ethanol-facts1.htm

5. Cook, Rob. "World Corn Production by Country." *Cattle Network*. Vance Publishing. 12 May 2009. Available at: http://www.cattlenetwork.com/World-Corn-Production-By-Country/2009-05-12/Article.aspx?oid=5017843

6. "Consumer Price Index – Average Price Data." United States Department of Labor. 16 Nov. 2009. Available at: http://data.bls.gov

7. "Corn boom may expand 'dead zone'." *MSNBC.com*. The Associated Press. 17 Dec. 2007. Available at: http://www.msnbc.com.msn.com/id/22301669

8. DeParle, Jason. "Hunger in U.S. at a 14-Year High." *NewYorkTimes.com*. 16 Nov. 2009. Available at: http://www.nytimes.com/2009/11/17/us/17hunger.html

9. "Ethanol's Federal Subsidy Grab Leaves Little for Solar, Wind and Geothermal Energy." *Environmental Working Group*. 8 Jan. 2009. Available at: http://www.ewg.org/reports/Ethanols-Federal-Subsidy-Grab-Leaves-Little-For-SolarWind-And-Geothermal-Energy+

10. "Ethanol Fuel." *Wikipedia.org*. 10 November 2009. Available at: http://en.wikipedia.org/wiki/Ethanol_fuel

11. "Ethanol Industry Statistics." Renewable Fuels Association. n.d. Available at: http://www.ethanolrfa.org/industry/statistics

12. "Frequently Asked Questions about Renewable & Alternative Energy Sources." Energy Information Administration. 29 July 2009. Available at: http://www.eia.doe.gov

13. Goldwert, Lindsay. "Indy 500 Goes From Gas to Green." *CBSnews.com*. 25 May 2007. Available at: http://www.cbsnews.com/stories/2007/05/25/eveningnews/main2853518.shtml

14. Holmseth, Timothy Charles. "Indianapolis 500 continues E100 use." *Ethanol Producer Magazine*. BBI International Media. 27 May 2008. Available at: http://www.ethanolproducer.com/article.jsp?article_id=4200&q=Indianapolis%20500&category_id=48

15. Knoll, Keith, Brian West, et al. "Effects of Intermediate Ethanol Blend on Legacy Vehicles and Small Non-Road Engines, Report 1 – Updated." National Renewable Energy Laboratory. February 2009. Available at: http://feerc.ornl.gov/pdfs/pub_int_blends_rpt1_updated.pdf

16. Layton, Julia. "Is Ethanol Really More Eco-Friendly than Gas?" *How Stuff Works*. n.d. Available at: http://auto.howstuffworks.com/fuel-efficiency/alternative-fuels/ethanol-facts1.htm

17. Lott Jr., John R. "Ethanol Mandates Cause Rising Food Prices." *FoxNews.com*. 28 April 2008. Available at: http://www.foxnews.com/story/0,2933,352968,00.html

18. Lyne, Jack. "Ethanol and Incentives: Fueling a Boon or a Boondoggle?" *Site Selection: Online Insider*. August 2007. Available at: http://www.siteselection.com/ssinsider/incentive/ti0708.htm

19. Lyon, Susan, Rebecca Lefton, and Daniel J. Weiss. "Quenching Our Thirst for Oil." *Center for American Progress*. 23 April 2010. Available at: http://www.americanprogress.org/issues/2010/04/oil_quench.html

20. Malkin, Elisabeth. "Thousands in Mexico City Protest Rising Food Prices." *NewYorkTimes.com*. 1 February 2007. Available at: http://www.nytimes.com/2007/02/01/world/americas/01mexico.html

21. Mandelbaum, Robb. "Life after Oil." *Discover Magazine*. 1 August 2006. Available at: http://discovermagazine.com/2006/aug/afteroil

22. "The Environmental Effects of Ethanol Production Plants: Citizens Responses." *Food First/ Institute for Food and Development Policy*. 6 July 2007. Available at: http://www.foodfirst.org/en/node/1713

23. "The Impact of Ethanol Use of Food Prices and Greenhouse-Gas Emissions." Congress of the United States: Congressional Budget Office. April 2009. Available at: http://www.cbo.gov/ftpdocs/100xx/doc10057/04-08-Ethanol.pdf

24. "The Rush to Ethanol: Not All Biofuels Are Created Equal." Food and Water Watch and Network for New Energy Choices. 2007. Available at: www.newenergychoices.org/uploads/RushToEthanol-rep.pdf

25. Thompson, Andrea. "Study: Corn ethanol will worsen 'dead zone'." *MSNBC.com*. Live Science. 2009. Available at: http://www.msnbc.msn.com/id/23695288

26. University of California – Berkeley. "Study: Ethanol Production Consumes Six Units of Energy To Produce Just One." *Science Daily*. 1 April 2005. Available at: http://www.sciencedaily.com/releases/2005/03/050329132436.htm

27. Wallace, Ed. "The Great Ethanol Scam." *Business Week*. Bloomberg. 14 May 2009. Available at: http://www.businessweek.com/lifestyle/content/may2009/bw20090514_058678.htm

chapter nine | BLOOD FOR OIL: CAFE STANDARDS

1. Balis, Ryan. "CAFE Standards Kill: Congress' Regulatory Solution to Foreign Oil Dependence Comes at a Steep Price." #546. *Nationalcenter.org*. National Policy Analysis. July 2006. Available at: http://www.nationalcenter.org/NPA546CAFEStandards.html

2. Coon, Charli. "Why the Government's CAFE Standards for Fuel Efficiency Should Be Repealed, not Increased." The Heritage Foundation. 11 July 2001. Available at: http://www.heritage.org/Research/Reports/2001/07/CAFE-Standards-Should-Be-Repealed

3. Crandall, Robert, Barry Felrice, Sam Kazman and Dr. W. David Montgomery. "Fuel Economy Standards: Do they Work? Do they Kill?" The Heritage Foundation. March 8, 2002. Available at: http://www.heritage.org/Research/Reports/2002/03/Fuel-Economy-Standards

4. Kazman, Sam. "Small Cars Are Dangerous Cars." The Wall Street Journal. 17 April 2009. Available at: http://www.knoxnews.com/news/2008/jan/28/nuke-fuel-recycling-project-a-spectacular-so-far/

5. Strzelczyk, Scott. "Congress, Toyota, and CAFE Standards." 26 Feb 2010. Available at: http://www.americanthinker.com/2010/02/congress_toyota_and_cafe_stand_1.html

chapter ten | CAP & TRADE: THE REAL STORY

1. Corsi, Jerome R. "Payoff! U.N. Climate Chief Cashes in on Carbon Scheme." *Wnd.com*. WorldNetDaily. 11 Dec 2009. Available at: http://www.wnd.com/index.php?fa=PAGE.view&pageId=118659

2. Dinan, Terry M. "The Distributional Consequences of a Cap and Trade Program for CO_2 Emissions." *Cbo.gov*. Congressional Budget Office. 12 March 2009. Available at: http://www.cbo.gov/ftpdocs/100xx/doc10018/03-12-ClimateChange_Testimony.pdf

3. Horner, Christopher. "Controlling hypocritical authority." *National Review*. 23 April 2002. Available at: http://www.nationalreview.com/comment/comment-horner042302.asp

4. Horner, Christopher. "Outside View: Caught En Flagrente Kyoto." *United Press International*. 31 Jan 2002. Print.

5. Kreutzer, David, Karen Campbell and Nicolas Loris. "CBO Grossly Underestimates Cost of Cap and Trade." *Heritage.org*. The Heritage Foundation. 24 June 2009. Available at: http://www.heritage.org/Research/energyandenvironment/wm2503.cfm

6. Kreutzer, David. "Discounting and Climate Change Economics: Estimating the Cost of Cap and Trade." *Heritage.org*. Web Memo: The Heritage Foundation. 19 Nov 2009. Available at: http://www.heritage.org/Research/EnergyandEnvironment/wm2705.cfm?renderforprint=1

7. Kreutzer, David W. "The Economics of Cap and Trade." The Heritage Foundation. 18 Sept 2008. Available at: http://www.heritage.org/cda/upload/KreutzerTestimonyTrade.pdf

8. Loris, Nicholas and Ben Lieberman. "Cap and Trade: A Handout for Corporations and a Huge Tax on Consumers." *Heritage.org*. Web Memo: The Heritage Foundation. No. 2476. 17 June 2009. Available at: http://www.heritage.org/research/energyandenvironment/wm2476.cfm

9. McCullagh, Declan. "Obama Admin: Cap and Trade Could Cost Families $1,761 a Year." *CBSNews.com*. 15 Sept 2009. Available at: http://www.cbsnews.com/blogs/2009/09/15/taking_liberties/entry5314040.shtml

10. Morgan, Dan. "Enron Also Courted Democrats." *The Washington Post*. 13 January 2002. Print.

11. Palin, Sarah. "The 'Cap And Tax' Dead End." *WashingtonPost.com*. The Washington Post. 14 July 2009. Available at: http://www.washingtonpost.com/wp-dyn/content/article/2009/07/13.html

12. Seper, Jerry. "Enron Gave Cash to Democrats, Sought Pact Help." *The Washington Times*. 16 January 2002. Print.

13. "The Cap and Tax Fiction." *WSJ.com*. The Wall Street Journal. 26 June 2009. Available at: http://online.wsj.com/article/SB124588827560750781.html

14. "The Climate Bill." *EnergyCitizens.org*. Energy Citizens. 2009. Available at: http://energycitizens.org/issues/the-climate-bill/

15. "The High Cost of Cap and Trade: Why the EPA and CBO Are Wrong." *Heritage.org*. The Heritage Foundation. 24 June 2009. Available at: http://www.heritage.org/press/factsheet/fs0034.cfm

16. Zubrin, Robert. "The Cost of Cap and Trade Bill." Roll Call News. 1 July 2009. Available at: http://www.rollcall.com/news/36393-1.html

chapter eleven | IF YOU ARE SERIOUS ABOU REDUCING CO$_2$, EMBRACE NUCLEAR POWER

1. "Processing of Used Nuclear Fuel." World Nuclear Association. Oct 2009. Available at: http://www.world-nuclear.org/info/inf69.html

2. "Reduce, Reuse, Recycle – Nuclear Waste?" *Roanoke.com.* The Roanoke Times. 25 Aug 2008. Available at: http://www.roanoke.com/editorials/wb/174362

3. "Electric Power Monthly." U.S. Energy Information Administration: Independent Statistics and Analysis. 15 Jan 2010. Available at: http://www.eia.doe.gov/cneaf/electricty/epm/epm_sum.html

4. Munger, Frank. "Nuke Fuel Recycling Project a 'Spectacular Success' So Far." *KnoxNews.com.* 28 Jan 2008. Available at: http://www.knoxnews.com/news/2008/jan/28/nuke-fuel-recycling-project-a-spectacular-so-far/

chapter twelve | A FINAL WORLD ON THE MAN-MADE GLOBAL WARMING HOAX

1. Hodge, Scott A. "Record Numbers of People Paying No Income Tax; Over 50 million "Nonpayers" Include Families Making over $50,000." Fiscal Facts. *Tax Foundation.* 10 Mar 2010. Available at: http://www.taxfoundation.org/publications/show/25962.html

2. Krosnick, Jon A. "The Climate Majority." *The New York Times.* 8 June 2010. Available at: http://www.nytimes.com/2010/06/09/opinion/09krosnick.html

3. Fineman, Howard. "What the Debate Should Be About." *Newsweek.* 1 Mar 2010. Available at: http://www.newsweek.com/id/234319/output/print

4. Ohlemacher, Stephen. "Nearly Half of US Household Escape Fed Income Tax." Associated Press. *Yahoo! Finance.* 7 Apr 2010.

5. Wolf, Richard. "Welfare Rolls up in '09; More Enroll in Assistance Programs." Gannet Co, Inc. *USA Today.* 26 Jan 2010. Available at: http://www.usatoday.com/news/nation/2010-01-25-welfare-rolls_N.htm

ABOUT THE AUTHOR

Richard C. Huseman, Ph.D. serves as an executive coach, keynote speaker, and consultant. He has had a variety of experiences in business school settings serving as professor, department head, and dean. Working with companies like AT&T, Coca Cola, ExxonMobil, Deloitte, Florida Hospital and IBM, his focus has been in the areas of knowledge management, Relational Intelligence®, change leadership, and leadership development.

Dick has authored 15 books, including his most recent works, **How The Brain Works: Unlock the Secret to Great Leadership**(2009), **Breakout: How to Unleash the Power of Human Capital** (2005), **The Leader As Coach: How To Coach A Winning Team** (2004) and, **Give-To-Get Leadership: The Secret of the Hidden Paycheck** (2002) as well as its precursor, **Managing The Equity Factor** (1989), which has been translated into Russian, German, Chinese, Portuguese, and Greek.

Man-Made Global Warming HOAX came out of concern about how little Relational Intelligence® is being leveraged in regard to several of the most critical issues facing the world today, most notably man-made global warming. It is this lack of Relational Intelligence® that inspires Dick to write about these issues to help inform and advise policy-makers and the public alike.

LaVergne, TN USA
15 August 2010
193363LV00001B